To Odie —

Who loves history and will enjoy the contents of this Book.

ove, Jean 8/6/82

# NEWPORT
## *PRESERV'D*

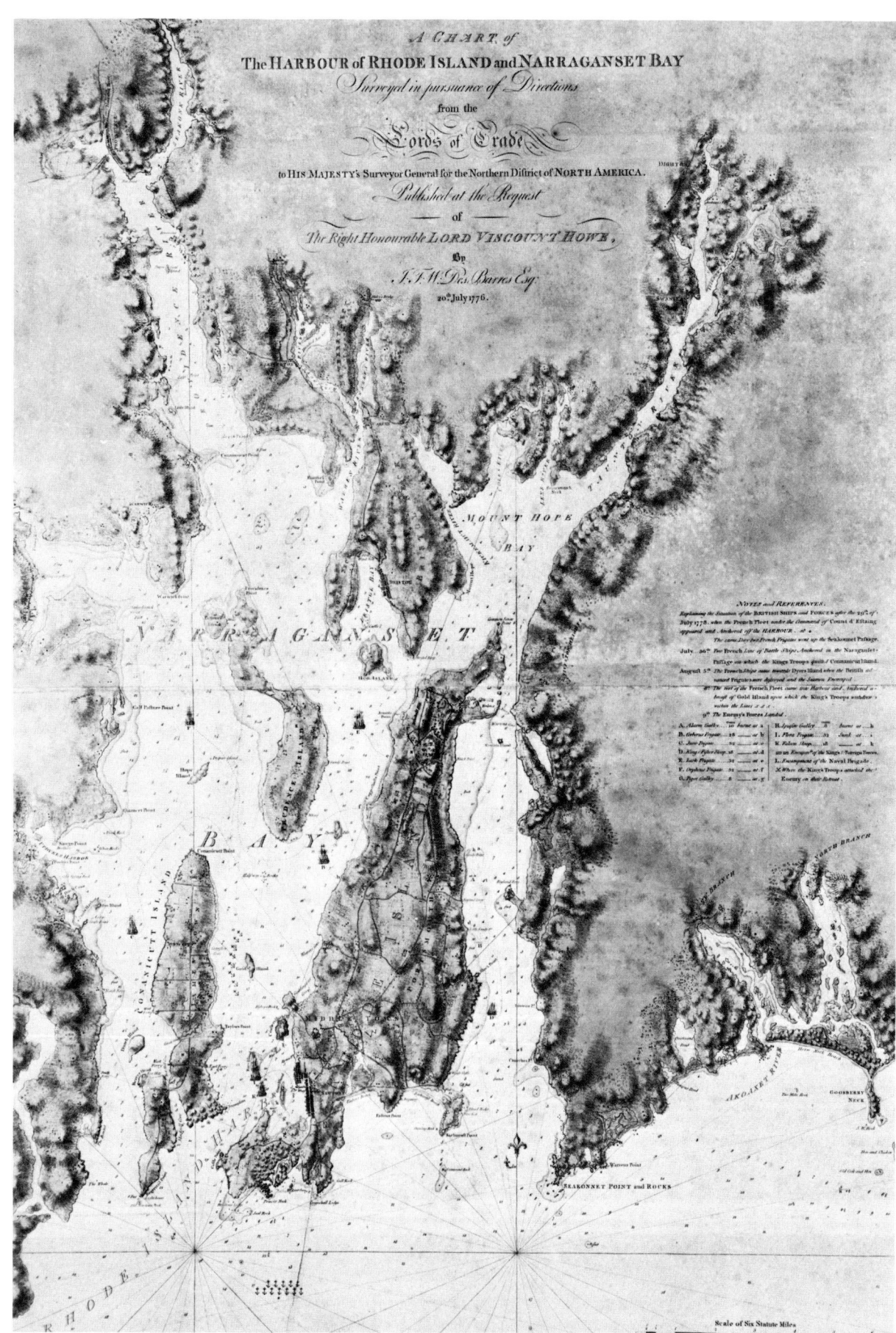

A Chart of the Harbour of Rhode Island and Narraganset Bay.
*Published by J. F. W. Des Barres, Esq., July 20, 1776.*

# NEWPORT PRESERV'D

## ARCHITECTURE OF THE 18th CENTURY

Desmond Guinness
Julius Trousdale Sadler, Jr.

A Studio Book · The Viking Press · New York

*To the ladies, God bless 'em!*

*Doris Duke*
The Newport Restoration Foundation

*The Hon. Nardine Pepys*
Operation Clapboard

*Katherine Warren*
The Preservation Society of Newport County

First published in 1982 by The Viking Press
(A Studio Book)
625 Madison Avenue, New York, N.Y. 10022
Published simultaneously in Canada by
Penguin Books Canada Limited

Library of Congress Cataloging in Publication
Data
Guinness, Desmond.
    Newport preserv'd.
    (A Studio book)
    Includes index.
    1.  Newport (R.I.)—Dwellings—
Conservation and restoration.
2.  Architecture, Domestic—Rhode Island—
Newport—Conservation and restoration.
3.  Architecture, Colonial—Rhode Island—
Newport— Conservation and restoration.
4.  Newport Restoration Foundation (R.I.)
I.  Sadler, Julius Trousdale.    II.  Title.
NA7238.N67G8      728.3′7′0288      81-11555
ISBN 0-670-50938-8                  AACR2

Printed in the United States of America
Set in Janson

# CONTENTS

# PROLOGUE: THE SEVENTEENTH CENTURY

THE SHORT-LIVED BURST OF eclectic emulation of European grandeur that epitomizes American architecture of the Gilded Age is an ebullient tributary of the mainstream of our architectural history. Its extravagances are perennially fascinating to serious student and casual observer alike. The name "Newport" is automatically associated with the splendors of Bellevue Avenue and Ocean Drive, where the great summer palaces of late nineteenth-century moguls still affirm the relish with which these worthies made—and spent—money. The names of these houses ring like a fanfare of massed bassoons: Belcourt, Ochre Court, Marble House, The Elms, The Breakers. Every year thousands of people come to wonder at them and, by paying for the privilege, help to maintain their expensive fabric.

It should be explained at the outset that this book is not about these stately nineteenth-century cottages, for their histories have been exhaustively documented, their undeniable appeal has been captured from every angle by brush and camera, and their unabashed opulence has long been a lodestone for the observer of the American panorama. This book is about the residences and public buildings of a much earlier day, when the Colonial city was perhaps our greatest seaport, and about their preservation and restoration. There has always been a concern in Newport for these earlier survivals, as well as for the Victorian heritage. The city has been the scene of a vigorous and praiseworthy effort, recently much intensified, to revive the beauty and aesthetic serenity of a pre-nineteenth-century approach to architecture and townscape.

This was an era when merchant shipping was the lifeblood of the Colonies, and a source of wealth to many Newport citizens.

Nor was conspicuous consumption on a grand scale unknown: one Quaker shipowner had a gold punch bowl made for him; enjoined by his faith from personal adornment, he expressed his yearning for magnificence in an artifact the like of which was not enjoyed by "the Queen herself." The old town of Newport is an archaeological resource so rich that is is sad that for many years it was virtually ignored save by scholars and antiquarians.

Colonial America subsisted off the land, but at first was forced to look to Europe for the very tools of that subsistence, and later for most of the luxuries that distinguish a pioneer existence from a less arduous way of life. Newport, founded in 1639 on one of the finest natural harbors on the Atlantic, was originally settled by nonconformist supporters of the "Antinomian heretic" Anne Hutchinson, who had left Boston for Portsmouth, Rhode Island, in 1638. In the following year William Coddington, Nicholas Easton, William Brenton, John Coggeshall, and John Clarke, with a score or so of fellows, withdrew from the Portsmouth settlement to the site of Newport. These were persons of substance and resource, and the community early came to support a prosperous middle class, from which many wealthy families sprang. The population grew from approximately 100 people in 1640 to 2,500 in 1680. These hard-working folk built sturdily and with increasing elegance, and although their earliest dwellings—grouped in clusters, with their individual gardens behind protective palisades—have long since been destroyed or altered beyond recognition, the number of seventeenth-century buildings surviving to the present day is remarkable.

Preservation, as the word is applied to architecture, is a curious phenomenon and takes many forms, from fortuitous neglect to comprehensive and meticulous reconstruction. It may be underwritten by public appeal, government agencies at various levels,

*Map of the old town area of Newport, where most of the buildings discussed here may be found.*

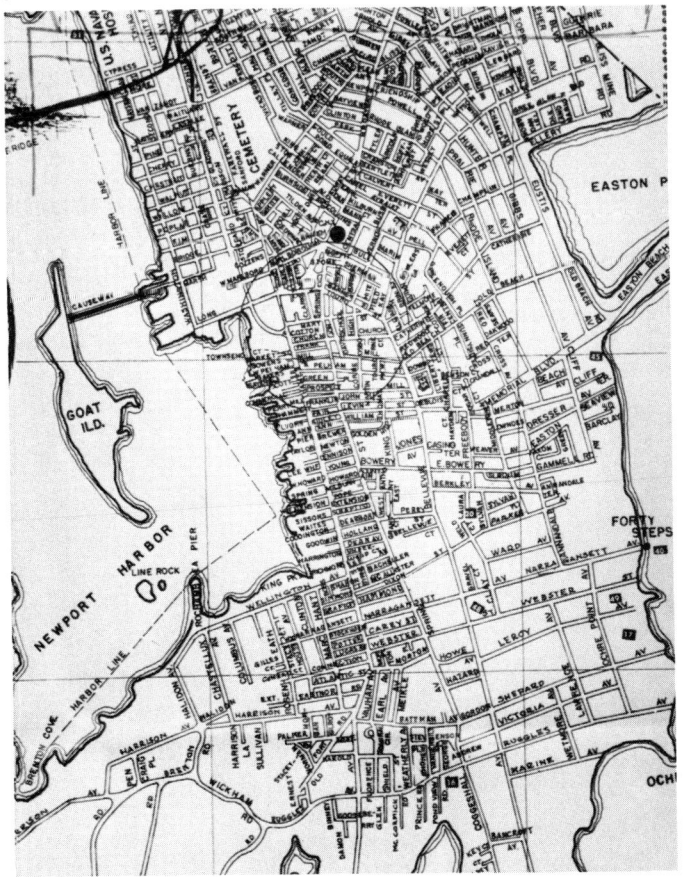

*Work in progress at the Newport Restoration Foundation workshops (top) and at 18 Thames Street (bottom).*

historical societies, civic associations, national and local organizations, private foundations, or concerned individuals. Its popularity has fluctuated, but historic preservation is an approved cause today, as American as apple pie, and those concerned with the welfare of early or otherwise important buildings are no longer generally regarded as eccentrics. The movement, much accelerated in recent years and ever more sophisticated in aims and technology, is not, however, new. There are approximately 350 pre-Revolutionary buildings in Newport proper, the greater part of which are now protected, preserved, or rehabilitated under one of the forms of sponsorship listed above.

In 1822 Abraham Touro set up a trust fund for the preservation of the eighteenth-century synagogue where his father, Isaac Touro, led the congregation. The Newport Historical Society, incorporated in 1854, has acquired and maintains both seventeenth- and eighteenth-century buildings, but many Colonial structures owe their continued existence to the long hiatus in Newport's urban growth, and to the Yankee predilection for making do. Some early houses form the upper stories of commercial establishments, having simply been raised to accommodate a new ground floor. Others have been buried under the accretions of the years, but with their primary structure left more or less intact. Still others were "restored" under the influence of various romantic theories in the nineteenth century. The latter are perhaps among the most difficult challenges to the modern preservationist.

The pioneer efforts of the Newport Historical Society have now been reinforced by the efforts of such like-minded organizations as the Preservation Society of Newport County, the Colonial Dames, The Society for the Preservation of New England Antiquities, The Rhode Island School of Design, the Foundation for the Preservation of America's Architectural Heritage,

*Concrete buttresses a stone foundation (top), and mantelpieces await reinstallation (bottom).*

Operation Clapboard and its successor, Oldport, Inc., and the Newport Restoration Foundation, Inc. These groups and institutions have bought up old houses and resold them to owners willing to restore them, or conducted the restoration work themselves and then sold or leased the buildings, or retained ownership and management and found self-sustaining uses for the properties.

The outcome of all this—and the work is still in progress—is a revitalized area containing more identified pre-Revolutionary houses than any other city on the Atlantic seaboard. The value of this astonishing treasure trove is tremendously enhanced by the fact that these buildings are largely in use. Quite a few are public buildings, commercial establishments, or museums open to the public. A greater number, built as residences, still serve their original purpose. Downtown Newport may look surprisingly well roofed, well pointed, and well painted for a relic of pre-Revolutionary times, but that is because it has been reestablished in its own continuum. It is an active, functioning community rather than a series of lovely shells from which the life has been carefully scrubbed away. To visit there today is to see a living present successfully integrated into a living past.

The earliest Newport houses were frame, with massive chimneys forming one stone end wall. These were simple, unpretentious dwellings, of a pattern common in Rhode Island, raised by the onerous labor of the owners and their friends. The "stone-enders" not only allowed room for a second fireplace, if desired, and a bread oven, but also formed a sort of radiant heat panel against the worst of the winter's cold. They were constructed with heavy timbers, following the medieval Gothic building systems still common currency among English carpenters, and were as simply finished within as was consistent with the stringencies of the climate. So little remains from this first period that it is impossible to pinpoint the date at which

*Top:* Newport Ruin. *Lithograph by W. G. Wall, ca. 1830. The village still lies mainly along the waterfront. In the background to the left is Fort Adams, and to the right is Fort Wolcott on Goat Island. Bottom: The Old Stone Mill, now surrounded by Touro Park. Opposite: The Elder John Bliss house, Bliss Road at Wilbur Avenue. The façade has been altered, but the stone end indicates its very early date.*

aesthetic ambition awoke. About 1670, perhaps, the first wide sheathing panels received a bevel at each edge after the piece was sawn. Turnings came later, but during the third quarter of the century, flat banisters were sawn into interesting shapes. The ice of stern necessity had begun to melt, and modest attempts to beautify interiors were made. Early carpenter-builders could hardly have imagined what an avalanche this impulse to embellish would become, or how much time, care, and expense would be lavished by future generations on the adornments of their homes.

Few of the original Rhode Island stone-enders remain. Governor William Coddington and Colony President John Coggeshall each put one up in 1641; neither survives. Governor Benedict Arnold, great-grandfather of the Revolutionary traitor, erected a stone-ender on Old Thames Street that stood until 1780. (Arnold is also said to have built the Old Stone Mill, the controversial truncated masonry tower that stands in Touro Park and which was for many years believed, on the frailest of evidence, to have been raised by Norsemen of the Vinland expedition. Latterly a theory has been put forward that it was the work of fifteenth-century Portuguese explorers, but it seems most likely that it was, after all, the base of Governor Arnold's windmill. Whatever its origin, it is certainly one of the very earliest European structures extant on these shores.) There is a stone-ender built by Eleazer Arnold in Lincoln, and in Newport itself is the Elder John Bliss house, standing at the corner of Bliss Road and Wilbur Avenue.

The house is not precisely dated, but it seems to have been built toward the end of the seventeenth century. It follows the Rhode Island "two room" plan, by which two fireplaces were set side by side in the end wall so that the introduction of a partition would conveniently divide the interior space longitudinally. The ceiling beams and corner

posts are chamfered in the medieval manner, but the stone chimney has been finished at the top with brick, which was not available to the earliest Newport masons. The original character of the house has been partially overlaid by eighteenth-century additions, although its fundamental design and structure is clear. It passed out of the Bliss family in 1807 and, having changed owners a time or two, was abandoned. Now restored, it is once again a private residence.

The White Horse, or Whitehorse, Tavern, parts of which were standing in 1673, is the oldest public house in terms of licensed operation in the United States. It was first opened by William Mayes, father of the notorious pirate William Mayes, in 1687. Always a popular gathering place, it has been much enlarged over the years, with most of the additions taking place during the eighteenth century. From the beginning, it was well placed for the regalement of the Society of Friends after Meeting in the days when small beer was a breakfast drink and wine was considered acceptable as a beverage, even for ladies. In 1713–14 the Town Council met there; the General Assembly used it pending the completion of the Colony House (q.v.), and out-of-town members stayed there, under the benevolent eye of host Jonathan Nichols, when the Assembly was in session.

Like many a long-lived hostelry, the White Horse suffered many vicissitudes, but was at last rescued, restored, and refurbished, and now operates as an up-to-date tavern, albeit in Colonial guise.

The Wanton-Lyman-Hazard house stands nearby, at 17 Broadway. Although it carries the names of three later owners, it was built about 1675 by Stephen Mumford for his own use. Mumford's work reflects that period in Colonial architecture when a primitive classicism was beginning to supplant the old Gothic concepts in building. The unchanged massive structural systems were by now being masked by paneled and chamfered work. This house displays another typical Newport (and New England) "two room" plan, having a single room on each side of a central chimney, with a fireplace opening into each. The chimney in this case is of brick rather than stone. The huge fireplaces have rounded sides, and the chimney has been given pilasters typical of the earliest Rhode Island practice. The steeply pitched roof is kicked out across the front to take a coved plaster cornice in a manner not commonly found in America. (A cornice of this kind is shown in Moxon's *Mechanic Exercises*, published in London in 1689.) Here it appears to be part of the original construction, contrived to resemble a classic cornice. The framework was originally all exposed, but the north chamber has now been restored so as to show the chamfered ceiling beams and gunstock corner posts. The vertical boarding of the sheathed walls is painted to imitate paneling, marbled in a kind of feather treatment using gray and dull red. Some early owner decorated the walls in a newer style, indicating that the old wide sheathing, perhaps painted plain red, had gone out of fashion. The walls of the kitchen lean-to, built early in the eighteenth century, were painted with a diamond crossbar in red on an ochre ground. A similar diamond design can be seen at 40 Division Street, in the rear stair hall of Augustus Lucas's house (q.v.). The pedimented front door was probably added by John Wanton in the eighteenth century, along with the sash windows and the mantel paneling.

Mumford sold his house in 1724 to Richard Ward, later a governor of the Colony, and by 1765 Martin Howard, Jr., was living there with Stamp Master Augustus Johnston. Howard was the bitter and outspoken author of the pro-British diatribe *A Letter from a Gentleman at Halifax*. In August 1765 word reached Newport of the passage of the Stamp Act, and an angry mob collected in front of the Colony House to hang in effigy three Tories: Howard, Johnston, and Dr. Thomas Moffatt, John Smibert's nephew and a friend of master builder Peter Harrison. Moffatt's part in publishing the pro-Royalist "O.Z." letters in *The Newport Mercury* of the early 1760s helped precipitate the storm provoked by the passage of the Stamp Act. The mob first reached Howard's house, where they smashed doors and windows as well as the furnishings. Dr. Moffatt's house suffered likewise, but Johnston's house survived almost unharmed. Howard and Moffatt made their escape on the British sloop *Cygnet*, which was then lying in the harbor. They never returned to Newport. A month later, John Wanton purchased the house at public auction and made the necessary repairs. The front door was probably installed by him at this time.

John Wanton's daughter married Daniel Lyman, and her father presented them with the house. Their daughter married Benjamin Hazard; the house remained in the Hazard family until 1927, when it was purchased by the Newport Historical Society. The architect Norman M. Isham undertook the restoration in that year. He ensured that as far as possible the varied architectural features of successive dates would all be preserved. Furnished in period, it is open to the public during the summer months, when visitors can see what is probably the oldest house still standing in Newport and one of the finest Jacobean-style residences in New England.

This handful of buildings almost completes the roster of pre-1700 houses to be seen today, but more survive than is at first apparent, concealed within eighteenth- and nineteenth-century modernizations.

Although little is now visible of Newport architecture of the seventeenth century, and although fashions and building systems changed and developed during the years that followed, the underlying pattern of the old town plan persisted long after the necessity for palisaded groupings had faded.

*The entrance hall of the
White Horse Tavern,
once the kitchen.*

Henry-Russell Hitchcock has pointed out that this was the layout from which the Great American Suburb evolved. Like other coastal cities, notably Charleston, Newport has managed to retain a little of the flavor of country living in the town. The streets are lined with largely wooden houses, each with its own yard or garden, however small. Like Charleston, too, Newport was for many years protected from the more devastating forms of progress by a cocoon of municipal and often personal poverty. The disruptions and damages of the Revolution put an end to prosperity, commerce, and even, it appeared to some, ambition, for hundreds of outstanding citizens fled the town.

What was destroyed in that conflict was a thriving, prosperous society that had enjoyed more than a century of almost uninterrupted growth, when all profitable sea-lanes led to Newport. A number of fortunes were founded on the "triangular" trade. In the days before conscience and economic reality in England and America had made the business illegal as well as indefensible, the swift merchantmen left Newport loaded with rum—distilled from West Indian molasses—and with gold. These were exchanged for slaves on the coast of Africa. The human livestock thus acquired was transported to the Caribbean and sold; with the proceeds, molasses was purchased and returned to New England to be converted to rum.

However, although the purchase of slaves from Africa was for many years perfectly legal, the direct purchase of molasses from Haiti was not, and Haiti was the most advantageous place from which to obtain it, since, to protect their brandy industry, the French masters of the island forbade the manufacture of rum there. The British government decreed that in order to reach the Colonies, Haitian molasses must first be shipped to France, exported to England, and resold to the Colonies, by which time it had,

*The White Horse Tavern before and after restoration. Unlike many Newport buildings, the tavern has never been moved from its original site at the corner of Farewell and Marlborough streets. Opposite: The White Horse Tavern.*

*Opposite: The Redwood Library. The statue of George Washington is a copy of the one by Houdon at the state capitol in Richmond, Virginia.*

*Above: The Almy-Taggart house. Left: Sampler by Roba White in the collection of the Newport Historical Society. Architectural motifs were prominent in early-nineteenth-century Rhode Island samplers.*

*Above: Whitehall.*
*Right: Doorway of the*
*Samuel Barker house*
*after restoration.*

*Above: The Brenton
farmhouse. Right:
Doorway of the John
Coddington house.*

*Above, left: The Samuel Whitehorne house.
Above: The central hall.
Left: The winter kitchen.*

*The Newport and Rhode Island furniture in the parlor of the Samuel Whitehorne house is accented by imported objets d'art. A tilt-top table with a triangular pedestal containing small drawers has its fellow in the Chippendale Bedroom at Winterthur.*

*Opposite: The Vernon house, where George Washington and General Rochambeau planned the victory at Yorktown.*

of course, become an expensive commodity. Various ingenious shifts were employed in bypassing this inconvenient regulation. During the French and Indian War, for example, according to John Millar, French prisoners of war were in great demand, as the presence of even one of them aboard a vessel made it a cartel ship, ostensibly bent on an exchange of prisoners, and thus guaranteed free access to the French colonial port of Haiti.

This trade also depended on an accommodatingly blind eye at His Majesty's Customs Office, but it must not be supposed that these excise officers, winking at the unloading of hogshead after hogshead of molasses that had certainly never seen a European warehouse, were essentially venal or dishonest men. Their complaisance was attributable to shortsighted British policies designed to wring every possible revenue from the Colonies at the expense of economic health, and the consequent impossibility of enforcing all these imposts without the presence of a standing army. (Later the Prohibition years were to reinforce the lesson that tariffs and exclusions, if generally believed to be unjust, will in general be ignored.) The Colonies might have risen in rebellion much earlier if every regulation intended to exploit them had been rigidly imposed.

Just as bootleggers under the Nineteenth Amendment expanded their operations into less savory or acceptable areas, so some Colonial shipmasters, having learned to flout unreasonable restrictions, slipped over the line into outright piracy. But by far the greater number of Colonial merchants and captains appear to have been God-fearing men of principle, even if their principles were sometimes at variance with the views of His Majesty's Government and with later conceptions of human rights. Newport, blessed with a salubrious climate, a splendid harbor, and more than its share of shrewd, courageous and industrious citizens, was by 1700 well on the way to achieving a proud place among Colonial cities.

Newport was a capital of Rhode Island, where the governor resided and the General Assembly met; the Colonial Naval Office was also located there. In addition to being, even then, a naval base, it was also, as has been noted, a major center for commercial shipping. Shipwrights, cordwainers, sail-makers, chandlers, smiths, coopers, and other tradesmen involved in the fitting and provisioning of the merchant fleet had more work than they could handle, and as they in turn prospered and the shipowners grew rich, the services of carpenters, masons, cabinetmakers, silversmiths, painters (of both walls and portraits), and clockmakers (in the intervals of supplying and adjusting chronometers for navigation) were much in demand to raise and furbish suitable dwellings. There was hardly a current trade, profession, or skill that was not represented among the owners and builders of documented houses in old Newport, and many among them are still noted, although their connection with Newport is sometimes forgotten.

Famous Newport artists and craftsmen include John Goddard, the Townsend family, and Holmes Weaver, who turned San Domingo mahogany, which had been brought from Haiti with the molasses, into furniture rivaling any produced in New York or Philadelphia. Clocks by William Claggett are coveted museum pieces. Gilbert Stuart, John and Nathaniel Smibert, Robert Feke, and the miniaturist Edward Green Malbone all lived and painted, at least for a time, in Newport. The work of half a dozen Newport silversmiths, such as William Hookey or Samuel Vernon, is some of the finest of the period. Richard Munday, self-styled housewright, is remembered for his part in erecting three of the finest public buildings in the city, and Peter Harrison, the gifted amateur architect of whom Fiske Kimball has said "Harrison was the forerunner, as Thomas Jefferson was the founder, of American classicism," both made meaningful contributions to the evolution of American architecture.

The Reverend Ezra Stiles, to whom we are indebted for a 1758 map of Newport (see page 127) and for many architectural notes and sketches, was for sixteen years pastor of the Second Congregational Church, before taking up his duties as president of Yale College. Dean—and later Bishop—Berkeley, the philosopher, poet, writer and educationist to whom Alexander Pope attributed "every virtue under heaven," spent three years in the area, making a host of friends, preaching in local churches, and, upon his unhappy departure, giving his thousand-volume library and his house in Middletown (q.v.) to Yale College. Rabbi Isaac Touro and his congregation founded the oldest surviving synagogue in the United States (q.v.), and a number of other well-known clergymen served in one or another of Newport's diverse houses of worship, exchanging pulpits upon occasion in a manner unheard of in that dogmatic time and far from common in this supposedly ecumenical age.

In 1780 the French forces, come to fight in the cause of American liberty, established headquarters in a Newport only lately evacuated by the British, who had occupied it almost since the outset of hostilities. For a year, therefore, the city hosted such luminaries as the marquis de Chastellux, the duc de Lauzun, and the comte de Rochambeau; it was then that George Washington visited Newport to plan and forward the latter conduct of the war by which these colonies became a nation.

The voices of a score of those who have left their imprint on our political, social, and aesthetic history still echo in the quiet rooms of Newport dwellings.

*Above: In the early 1970s the Wanton-Lyman-Hazard house, 17 Broadway, had three dormers in the roof. These have since been removed (left).*

# CATALOGUE: THE EIGHTEENTH CENTURY

**B**Y THE BEGINNING OF THE 1700s increasing trade and consequent growth had brought a building boom to Newport. From the turn of the century, houses of consequence began to appear in numbers. Some were planned and constructed all of a piece, as it were; many others were extrapolated from earlier, smaller homes that had failed to allow space for a less necessitous and more expansive life.

Jahleel Brenton's 1720 house was one of the first great houses to be built in Newport in which the developed academic plan of central hall, four rooms, and two chimneys was used. (This is also the plan of the Vernon house [q.v.], but in that instance the plan evolved in the remodeling.) The distinctive gable-on-hip roof, the symmetrical façade, and the tall and narrow windows were all characteristic of the Palladian style as introduced into England by Inigo Jones. The Brenton house is gone, but some of its woodwork was removed before it was demolished. The parlor paneling, which was preserved by The Rhode Island School of Design, was unfortunately lost in the fire that destroyed the second floor of The Breakers stable, where it had been stored for safekeeping. Only the staircase remains to remind us of that once lovely interior.

The Vernon house, at the corner of Clarke and Mary streets, is one of several eighteenth-century Newport residences to incorporate an earlier and much more modest dwelling in its ample composition. The original house was of two and one-half stories, with a single chimney, but when in 1759 it changed hands, its size was doubled and more, and it received its present façade and finish, making it one of the handsomest among a score or more fine Colonial homes to be seen in the vicinity today. The rebuilding

*Top: Paneling in the parlor of the Jahleel Brenton house, 1720. Above: Sawn baluster staircase from the Micah Spencer house, ca. 1720. The house stood at 87 Thames Street, but was torn down in 1940.*

appears to have been the work of Peter Harrison. The blocked wooden exterior, sanded to look like stone, is one of his signatures, and the balance and detail of the façade suggest his feeling for classic values.

In 1937 some murals in the Chinese taste were accidentally discovered behind later paneling in the older part of the house. There is a series of panels, framed with simulated bolection moldings, displaying scenes from the Chinese courts of punishment and the Buddhist hell, all executed in gold and yellow on a black ground. These paintings have been carefully restored, and the paneling overlaying them has been hinged so that they may be rediscovered without difficulty. They are presumed to date from between 1725 and 1740 and, from the accuracy of their Oriental style, appear to have been done by someone who had visited the Far East.

A West Indian scene was discovered in 1879 behind the paneling of the chimney breast in an upper room, but it was removed from the house and its whereabouts cannot now be traced. The rest of the house contains excellent circa-1758 paneling, but this must perforce take second place to the exceptional interest of the Chinese wall paintings.

General Washington visited the house in 1781, when it was the temporary headquarters of General Rochambeau, commander in chief of the French allies during the Revolution. It was apparently Rochambeau who built the one-story ballroom in the garden which appears in several engravings and early photographs. The cornice of the ballroom matched that of the house, but the ballroom has been taken down, and there is a later building on the site.

The rear entrance of the Augustus Lucas house, at 40 Division Street, was originally a front door, and it gives onto a wooden staircase with flat sawn banisters and a closed string course (i.e., the ends of the steps are concealed—see illustration). Seen from Division Street, the square house appears to

*Above: The Rhoades-Pease-King house, 32 Clarke Street, dates from the early eighteenth century. The pilastered chimney and kick at the eaves indicate its early date and its kinship to the Wanton-Lyman-Hazard house. Left: Later alterations for a time concealed its original lines.*

The Vernon house, at the corner of Clarke and Mary streets. The original small dwelling was to the left, on the north end.

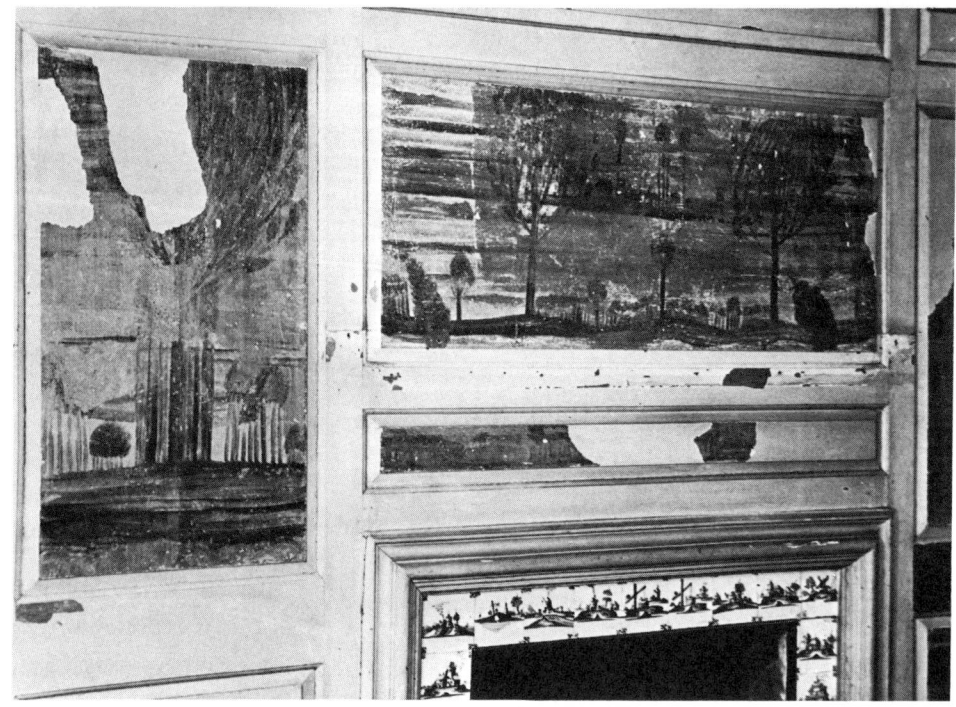

*Above: The north parlor of the Vernon house, showing the paintings in the Chinese taste. Right: Murals in the northwest bedroom, over the north parlor.*

Left: A detail of the Chinese murals. Below: An early photograph of Clarke Street. The Vernon house and the "Frenchman's Ballroom" are to the right; the former Second Congregational Church, of which Ezra Stiles was minister, is on the left. When the Central Baptists purchased this 1735 building, it was enlarged and brought into the then current mid-nineteenth-century Greek Revival mode.

*Right: Now at 18 Denison Street, this house was moved from West Broadway. It appears to have first been used as a Baptist meeting house before being made into a residence about 1710. Below: The house before it was moved.*

Top: The brick end-section on the left side of this house at 109 Spring Street was added to an earlier nucleus sometime after 1705. The building was later altered to form a double house, and around 1788 it was used as a Quaker boys' school. Below, left: The house restored to how it might have looked when it was owned by Major John Otis, silversmith. Bottom: Porringer made by Otis, and now in the collection of the Newport Historical Society.

*The Augustus Lucas house stands at the corner of Division and Mary streets, in the Hill section.*

be a gable-on-hip-roofed house of about 1750, but in fact, as in the Vernon house, parts of it are much older. Lucas, a French Huguenot, arrived in Newport from St.-Malo in 1698, after having spent some time in the Channel Islands. The Boston *News Letter* for 1711 carried an advertisement for Indian and Negro slaves for sale, to be "seen at the house of Augustus Lucas." In that year Lucas purchased the lot on the corner of Division and Mary streets, and shortly thereafter bought the lot adjoining. By 1721 there was a record of buildings, as well as an orchard where Lucas experimented in grafting fruit trees. The front part of the existing house is

*A doorway being returned to its place in the Dr. David King house at 34 Pelham Street after years of use elsewhere. Above: The house as it was before its recent restoration. It had been extensively altered since it was built in 1711. Above, right: The King house after restoration. The interior displays a finely detailed stairway and handsome mantels. Dr. King was a pioneer in the treatment of yellow fever. Right: Interior view of the restored King house.*

*Doorway of the Samuel Barker house, 119 Spring Street, ca. 1714; it is shown here before the house was restored. This house has brick ends below its gambrel roof; brick was rarely used in Newport at that time (it was not manufactured locally) except in the construction of chimneys, but in built-up neighborhoods the masonry ends offered some protection against fire.*

*Opposite, above: The Daniel Carr house at 20 Division Street, ca. 1712. Its wide overhanging cornice, heavy exposed beams, sawn balusters, and large keeping-room fireplace with a bake oven within it indicate the early date of the house. Note the juxtaposition of clapboard and shingle in the siding. End walls were often covered in cheaper materials than the front, hence the expression "Queen Anne front and Mary Ann behind."*

*Right: The house at 6 Cross Street, Easton's Point, ca. 1713, was built for Thomas Walker but about 1733 became a tavern, the King's Arms. The roof resembles that of the Carr house. It has a large central pilastered brick chimney with three fireplaces on each floor. The ground-floor fireplaces, like those of the White Horse Tavern and the Wanton-Lyman-Hazard house, have rounded side walls and a cove above the chimney beam.*

*Entrance of the restored Samuel Barker house in Christmas dress. Once divided into apartments, the house is now a single private residence again.*

obviously later than 1721, but the rear staircase may well date from that time. These stairs, set in a cramped position between the outer door and the chimney, were built in three short runs with windows and corner posts; their design is one common in early New England homes—six or seven staircases of this type survive in Newport. Wall decoration in a red diamond pattern on a dark ground may still be seen on the stair wall in the garret; it resembles the painting in the ell of the Wanton-Lyman-Hazard house, and may be by the same hand.

Augustus Johnston, Lucas's grandson, came into the property before 1765, and was probably responsible for the enlargement, as stylistic evidence shows that it must have been remodeled sometime in mid-century. There is a modillion cornice and an Ionic pedimented doorway; spiral balusters support the ramped railing of the front stairs. The rooms to either side of the hall on both floors have retained their original raised paneling on the chimney breasts.

Unfortunately for himself, in 1765 Johnston accepted the post of Stamp Master. As mentioned earlier, rioters protesting the "intolerable" new Stamp Act stormed Johnston's house, while he took refuge in the cellar. He and the house survived, but he soon resigned his office and left Newport for Charleston, where he became Judge of the Admiralty Courts.

Johnston's stepfather, Matthew Robinson, bought the house in 1766. There has since been a succession of owners, but the house is basically little changed, although it had become so dilapidated by 1960 that it was condemned by the municipality. It was rescued in the nick of time by a consortium of purchasers, and is now restored and protected.

Close by, at 46 Division Street, is the house of Dr. Samuel Hopkins, built about 1751. A vigorous opponent of slavery who had studied theology with Jonathan Edwards, he came to Newport to serve as minister of the First Congregational Church in 1770 and lived in the house until his death in 1803. The house has its gambrel end facing the street, and an old photograph shows it with louvered shutters at the windows; these have since been removed.

Hopkins not only preached against the slave trade but raised money to obtain the freedom of many slaves and hoped to establish colonies for them in Africa. That dream was never realized, but his influence and that of Newport's other spiritual leaders—Quaker, Episcopalian, and Congregational—eventually prevailed. Long before the abolition of slavery became an issue sufficiently vital to divide the nation almost permanently, Newport had freed its slaves. In 1834, the Union Congregational Church, the first free black church in America, was erected, quite fittingly, on Division Street.

GEORGE BERKELEY LANDED AT "NEW Port" on January 23, 1729. He was a Senior Fellow of Trinity College, Dublin, Dean of Derry, and would later become Bishop of Cloyne. He had published, in 1725, *A Proposal for the Better supplying of Churches on our foreign plantations, and for converting the Savage Americans to Christianity, by a College to be erected on the Summer Islands, otherwise called the Isles of Bermuda.* He was promised £20,000 for the undertaking, and set sail with his bride for Rhode Island in 1728. In the party were his wife's friend "my Lady Handcock's daughter"; John Smibert, who became one of America's first professional artists; Duguize, a musician; two gentlemen of fortune; and a number of tradesmen.

Dean Berkeley arrived in a Newport already enjoying the beginnings of an intellectual and aristocratic society. He also found "four sorts of Anabaptists, besides Presbyterians, Quakers, Independents

*Opposite: The Samuel Hopkins house, 16 Division Street. Above: The house in an old photograph.*

and many of no profession at all." Notwithstanding so many differences, "here are fewer quarrels about religion than elsewhere, the people living peaceably with their neighbors of whatever persuasion. They all are agreed on one point, that the Church of England is second best."

Soon after his arrival Berkeley bought a farm about three miles from Newport and enlarged the small house on it, which he christened "Whitehall," to accommodate the needs of his household. True to his convictions, he followed the dictates of Palladio as best he could in his remodeling. The entrance appears to have been inspired by the Ionic doorcase shown in Plate 56, Volume I, of *The Designs of Inigo Jones*,

Opposite, above: The Quaker Meeting House at the corner of Farewell and Marlborough streets; lithograph by John Collins, ca. 1857. The original meeting house, built in 1700 with a turret and hip roof, has been incorporated in the center of the building. Left: Photograph of the meeting house before restoration; the later wing seems to dwarf the main structure behind it.

Opposite, below: This lithograph by William Dane was published after the 1852 addition of the projecting wing. The details are in the fashionable Greek Revival style. Left: The Quaker Meeting House in 1980.

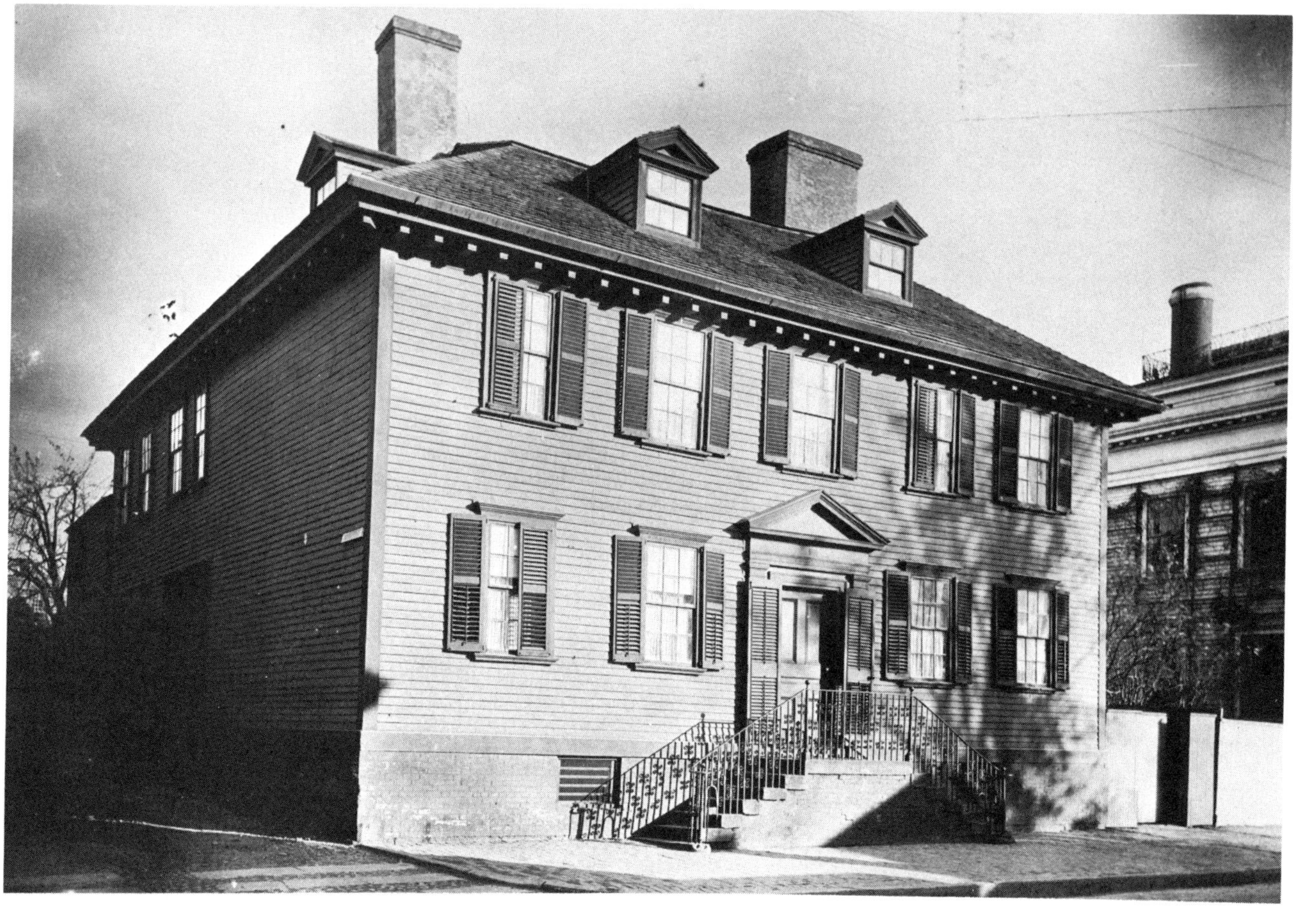

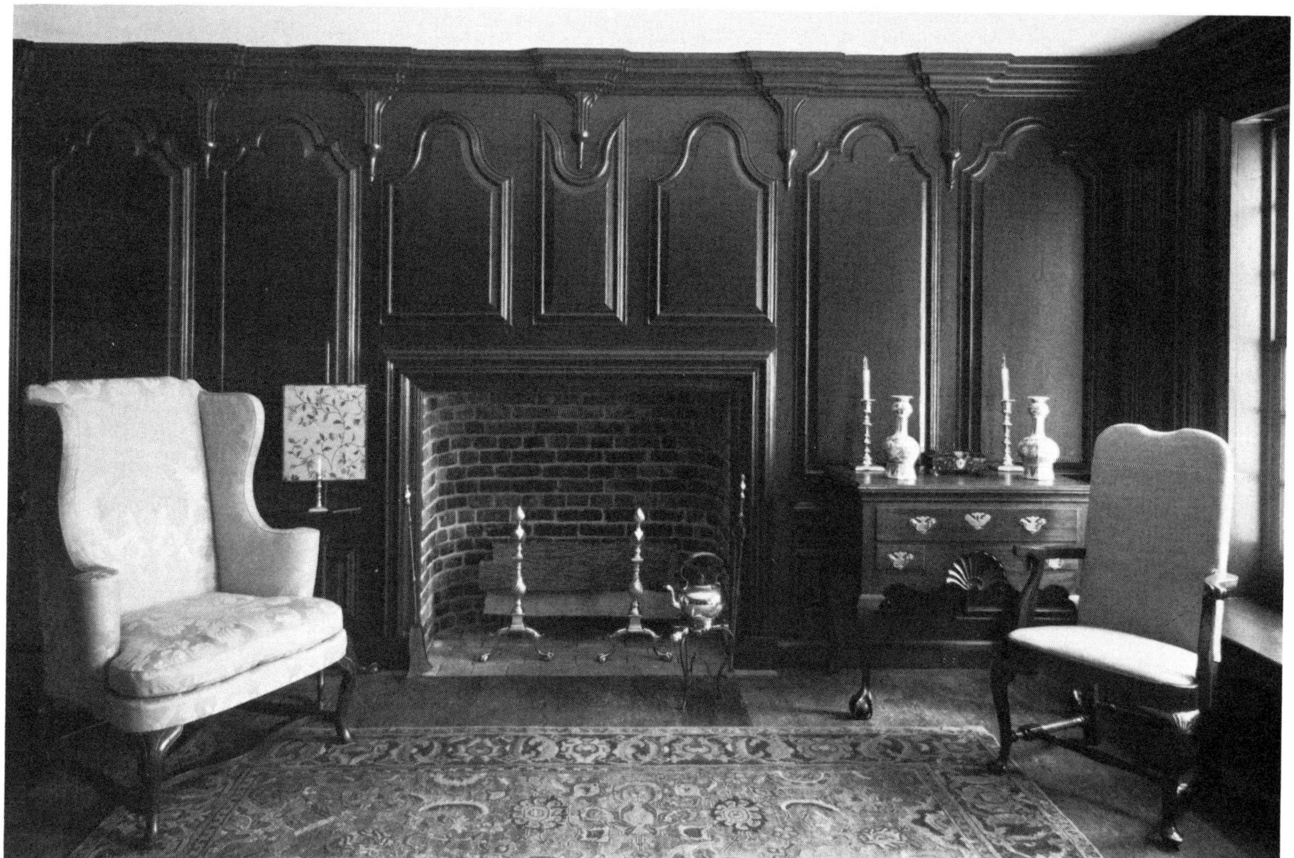

*Opposite, above: The John Gidley house, 1724, stood
at the corner of Thames and Gidley streets. It has
been demolished, but some of the interior woodwork
was rescued and has been used in other houses.
Below: The north parlor interior of the house was at
one time installed in the home of the architect
George Champlin Mason. It was later moved to
Winterthur and lowered to its original height; an
extra row of panels had been inserted above the chair
rail to adapt its eighteenth-century proportions to the
height of Mason's nineteenth-century ceiling.
Above: The Caleb Claggett house, 22 Bridge Street,
ca. 1725. It has brick ends, still uncommon at the
time, and is braced with iron tie rods ending in the S.
The front is not symmetrical, but the front door is
centered before the central chimney. The builder was
father to William Claggett, the clockmaker, who
lived next door at 16 Bridge Street.*

*Above: Christopher Townsend's house and shop, 74 Bridge Street, ca. 1725; the first of the group of houses built by the Townsend and Goddard families. Christopher Townsend was a ship's cabinet-maker. Right: The stairway, carved by Christopher Townsend. Townsend-Goddard furniture is still cherished by individuals and sought by museums.*

*Whitehall, Dean Berkeley's Newport home. In 1973 the National Society of the Colonial Dames of America in the State of Rhode Island and Providence Plantations purchased the remaining interest of the Whitehall leasehold from Yale.*

which had been published by William Kent in 1727. This work would have been familiar to him at Trinity, and he may even have owned a copy. He was particularly interested in doors, discoursing on their proportions in his long poetic work *Alciphron*, written at Whitehall. In order to achieve the correct proportions for the front door, he had to make the left panel blind, with a solid wall behind it. This modest doorcase may be the first expression of the Palladian idiom to find its way to New England. It is chaste by comparison with the provincial baroque doorways of Trinity Church and the Colony House, with their naïve scroll pediments. The interior layout is unexceptional, with rooms on either side of a central lobby and across the back under the saltbox roof.

The promised funds for his college were not forthcoming; Berkeley returned to England in 1731. He remembered his sojourn in the New World with affection, and sent an organ to Trinity Church, where he had preached often, as well as presenting his library and Whitehall itself to Yale College. The income from the house was directed to the support of "three deserving students." By 1743 Whitehall had become an inn, and a popular halting place for summer visitors. By the end of the century it was derelict, but in 1899 the Colonial Dames of America obtained a 999-year lease on the ruinous building—then still owned by Yale—and began a program of preservation and restoration, including an eighteenth-century garden. Once again it welcomes summer visitors.

Richard Munday, innkeeper and house carpenter, is also the first architect to be identified among the hitherto faceless builders and craftsmen who worked in Newport. The first building he is known to have designed, Trinity Church, is also his masterpiece. Trinity, center of the oldest Episcopal parish in New England, is one of the glories of Newport and the nation.

The Bermuda Group, *by John Smibert; George Berkeley and his family, with the painter shown standing at the far left.*

*The front entrance at Whitehall. The left panel of the door is false.*

The original church, built in 1702, proved inadequate for the growing congregation, and in 1726 Munday was commissioned to replace it with a larger one. It is a combination of a "mass house" and a "preaching house"—of a long church with the altar at the east end and a broad assembly room built for preaching, with the pulpit in the center of the long side. The altar from the 1702 church, an oak table of William and Mary type with curved stretchers and turned and twisted legs, is still in use. The boxed pews are arranged to form little rooms for worshipers, paneled in pine and painted white. To start with, they were stained a dark color, providing a visual anchor for the white plaster walls and ceiling. There are those who would prefer to see the color scheme put back to the original, but the pews have been white now for as long as anyone can remember, and the congregation is averse to change. Some clumsy stained glass has been allowed to intrude, but not enough to spoil the generally light and happy effect. The spire was erected in the 1740s, after Munday's death, to his design. It is based on the Wren-inspired spire of Christ Church, Boston, and is one of two in the United States still surmounted by a crown.

In 1762 the church was lengthened, by the insertion of two bays, and the wine-glass pulpit was moved to dominate the central aisle. The windows in this extension are of cedar, whereas those in the rest of the building are pine; the great arched window above the altar is also cedar and presumably dates from this period. Dean Berkeley's organ, made by Robert Bridges of London, arrived at Trinity in 1733, the second such instrument to have come to North America. The central part of the case is original, but the pipes have been replaced, and the first keyboard, supposedly touched by Handel, is in the care of the Newport Historical Society. A gilded royal crown and twin miters surmount the case. Norman Isham, who restored Trinity,

*Above: The Green Parlor, to the left of the Whitehall lobby. The room has retained its bolection-paneled chimney breast. Right: An advertisement from* The Newport Mercury, *June 11, 1764. Opposite, above: Whitehall, ca. 1837, from the sketch by Lieutenant A. A. Harwood, U.S.N., prepared for the book* Picturesque Illustrations of Rhode Island, and the Town of Newport. *Opposite, below: Whitehall, in a photograph from the* New York Sketch Book of Architecture, *1874.*

## Amos Whiting,

Has juſt opened a TEA-HOUSE at WHITE-HALL, where he deſigns to entertain Gentlemen and Ladies in a genteel Manner, whoſe Cuſtom is deſired, and will be eſteemed a ſingular Favor——Good Paſturing for Cattle at the ſame Place, at a reaſonable Rate.

Drawn by A. A. Harwood.

*Front View of Whitehall near Newport*

*Formerly the residence of Dean Berkley and given by him to Yale College.*

*Opposite: Interior of Trinity Church, Spring Street, from the organ loft. George Washington occupied Pew 83 (to the left of the pulpit) when he visited Newport in 1781. Beyond is Smyth's monument. Right: Trinity Church.*

has suggested that the gallery where the choir sits may have been broken forward to accommodate this organ. Munday was summoned from Bristol to supervise its installation.

The church contains some interesting marble monuments, notably that on the left of the altar to the memory of the Reverend Marmaduke Browne, rector 1760–61, erected by his son Arthur in 1795, and carved in Dublin by J. Smyth. Smyth was responsible for all the best sculptures on the main public buildings of the time in Dublin, such as the Custom House and the Four Courts.

*The Reverend James Honyman, rector of Trinity Church, was appointed in 1704 and remained with the congregation until his death in 1750. The mezzotint engraving, after a portrait by Gaines, was printed by Reak and Okey in Newport in 1774. Opposite: Queen Anne Square before it was cleared. The Dr. Charles Cotton house can be seen in its original position at the lower left.*

QUEEN ELIZABETH II CAME TO Newport in 1976 and formally christened the newly created square below Trinity Church "Queen Anne Square." It was laid out through the generosity of the Newport Restoration Foundation, Inc., in place of a degraded cluster of neon-fronted stores; the establishment of large trees and shrubs could not be undertaken until these had been removed. The great work of planting was finally accomplished in the fall of 1978, and several of the houses rescued by the Foundation have been moved to form the sides of the square.

Dr. Charles Cotton's was until recently the only house remaining on the old wide building line of Thames Street. It is shown as originally sited on Ezra Stiles's map of 1758. Part of Cotton Court, it stood in the midst of twentieth-century stores and parking lots. It was moved in 1978 by the Newport Restoration Foundation and now faces Queen Anne Square.

The front door opens onto a stairway, behind which there is a central chimney serving the principal rooms. The room to the right of the hall has as its chief decorative feature an eagle worked in plaster in the center of the ceiling. Unique in Newport, this plasterwork is without a doubt a later embellishment, added after the federal eagle became an important emblem in the new Republic.

The Erastus Pease house (ca. 1785), still a private residence, stands at 36 Church Street, just to the east. It has what is for Newport an unusual roof line; instead of a simple gable or gambrel, the Pease house has become known as "the house with the Pagoda roof." The gambrel drops down and curves sharply at the bottom, creating a wide soffit. Otherwise, it resembles the Cotton house next door; the rooms are ranged on either side of a central hall, with the original kitchen behind.

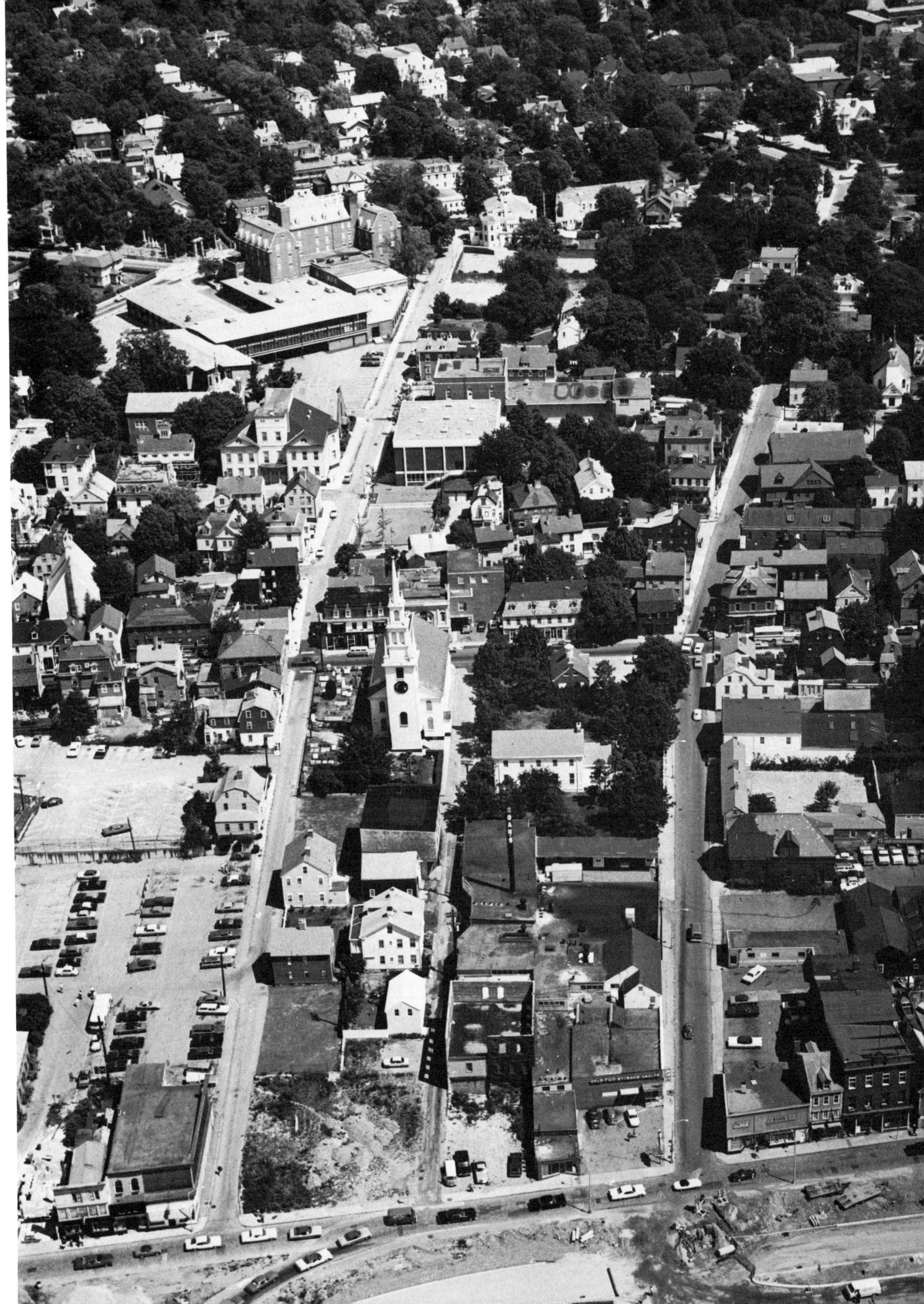

*Above: Queen Anne Square in 1980. Right: Trinity Church faces the top of the open green. In the center are Dr. Cotton's house and the Erastus Pease house.*

*Above: Dr. Cotton's
house before its removal
from Cotton Court.
Right: Stages in
removal and
restoration. At its new
site at 32 Church Street,
the house acquired
dormers.*

*The Erastus Pease house, 36 Church Street.*

The house now located at 77 Bridge Street was moved to the site from 5 Charles Street. Originally, however, it had occupied the corner of Charles Street and Washington Square, where land records show it before 1726. In that year Jonathan Chace, mariner, purchased a "lot of land with a messuage or dwelling house." The present house, doubled in size in about 1744, has a typical gambrel roof. There is a pedimented door leading into the central hall, but because of the early structure, the façade is not symmetrical. The little stairway with S-shaped balusters, rising in three tight runs, and the framing for the mammoth chimney belong to this earlier period.

Sometime after 1742 Ebenezer Flagg and his bride, Mary Ward, settled in the house, which may have been given to them as a wedding present. Mary Ward was the daughter of Governor Richard Ward and the niece of merchant Henry Collins, the previous owner of the house. Collins was called the Lorenzo de' Medici of Rhode Island because of his patronage of arts and letters. He is associated with the construction of Touro Synagogue, and he gave the land upon which the Redwood Library now stands. He is thought to have been responsible for the stylish expansion of the house. One John Stevens, mason, laid down paving and steps, and altered the chimney and fireplace by setting up ninety-five tiles, possibly the Dutch tiles then so much in vogue. The original half-a-house, with its end chimney, became the central-chimneyed house that stands today; the inventory of Flagg's personal property taken after his death in 1762 shows that the additions had been completed by then.

Flagg was a founding member of the Redwood Library. He was engaged in the manufacture of cordage and later became associated with Collins in shipping. For a space the firm prospered, but the difficulties in the 1750s caused by the Seven Years' War forced the firm into bankruptcy.

*Below: Notice in* The Newport Mercury, *May 17, 1773. Bottom: Pitt's Head Tavern when it was at 5 Charles Street. Its original location on the Parade may be seen in the 1840 illustration on page 81.*

**Robert Lillibridge, jun.**

At the sign of PITT's head, near the Court-house, NEWPORT,

Hereby informs the public, that he has now in good order,

A Genteel COACH, coachman, and two good horses, for carrying out gentlemen and ladies on parties of pleasure.—The coachman understands driving well, and waiting on company in the best manner; and will attend at the houses of any gentlemen and ladies with the coach, at any hour they may chuse.

This coach will carry four persons comfortably, and the expence to each will be but a trifle more than that of riding in a chaise: Whoever will be pleased to employ said coach, may depend on being treated in the most obliging manner, and have their favours very gratefully acknowledged. (66)

Mary Flagg sold the house in 1765 to Robert Lillibridge. Soon afterward he hung out the "Sign of the Right Honorable William Pitt's Head," and the house entered upon a long and colorful career as a coffeehouse. The likeness of William Pitt, "the Great Commoner," had originally come from an establishment run by a James Brooks on Thames Street. Opened in 1759, his coffeehouse closed within the year, but the new Pitt's Head thrived under Lillibridge's ownership. He advertised in *The Newport Mercury*, which also advertised Whitehall as a "Tea House" in the 1760s and '70s.

During the Revolutionary War, the tavern was occupied by British, Hessian, and lastly French soldiers. In the early part of the nineteenth century, the Collector and the Naval Officer for the Port of Newport had their offices here. Edward Lawton bought it

*Pitt's Head Tavern,
now at 77 Bridge Street.
The railing that
surrounded the gambrel
roof has been removed.*

in 1815, and in 1877 the Lawton family sold it
to the Independent Order of Odd Fellows.
They moved it to the rear of the lot to make
room for their new hall, and turned the house
to face Charles Street. Eventually the tavern
was purchased by the Preservation Society of
Newport County, and partially restored
under the direction of John Perkins Brown. It
has since passed again into private hands and
been moved to its present location, where it is
a family residence.

As late as 1750 it was reported that there
were in Newport only two brick buildings;
the Colony House was one, and Godfrey
Malbone's mansion the other. Malbone came
to Newport from Queen Anne County in
Virginia about 1700, and amassed a fortune in
the slave trade. His house, which stood at the
corner of Thames and Cannon streets, was
almost certainly designed by Richard
Munday. The 1740 *View of Newport* shows
the house as a gambrel-roofed edifice with a
balcony, dormers, roof balustrade, and cupola.
It apparently much resembled another noted
seaport mansion, the John Hancock house,
which was erected on Beacon Hill in Boston
in 1737. Malbone spared no expense in the

*Captain Peter Simon house, 25 Bridge Street, ca. 1727. Its gable-on-hip roof surmounts a later house than the original; the doorway in the Palladian taste was put in after 1800. It was to this house that the "unfortunate Hannah Robinson" came as a bride with Peter Simon, Jr., her dancing master, whom she married against her father's wishes; she was, in fact, deserted in a short time.*

adornment of his home. In 1728 John Fletcher, painter, sent Malbone a bill for £50 for twenty-five thousand leaves of gold for "gilding the Great Room and the spout heads." Fletcher charged £5 for the trip to Boston to obtain the gold leaf. The records of John Stevens, stoneworker (q.v.), show that in 1749 he cut and set a marble chimney piece for Malbone. One of the mantels from the house is now in the Newport Historical Society together with many other treasures of vanished early Newport, chief of which is the Sabbatarian Meeting House.

The Sabbatarian Meeting House (1729) bears the stamp of Richard Munday's style although it was put up under the direction of Jonathan Weeden and Henry Collins. Its similarity to Trinity attests the completeness with which a dissenting congregation had adopted the style of the new Episcopal churches, as Antoinette Downing has pointed out. It would seem likely that the same men must have worked at Trinity Church three years before, as the paneling and moldings are so similar. Originally, twisted banisters—like those still to be found in the Meeting House—led up to the Trinity pulpit. There is

*A reconstruction by John Millar of the elevation of the vanished Godfrey Malbone house.*

a gallery, and the wine-glass pulpit, originally surmounted by a carved and gilded crown, is in the center of the long wall. In the nineteenth century the pews were removed, and the paneling around the walls was made out of them.

The Sabbatarians disbanded in 1835. Fifty years later the building was moved from Barney Street to Touro Street and placed in the care of the Newport Historical Society. It was restored by George Champlin Mason in 1884, and again under the care of Norman Isham in 1916. The exterior brick veneer is a 1915 protective addition. A remarkable 1731 clock made by William Claggett is attached to the gallery opposite the pulpit, suitably positioned to remind the preacher of the passing minutes; it has kept time in that spot since it was first installed. Claggett came to Newport from Boston in 1716. In that year, one William Randall was advertising his expertise in lacquerwork in that city, but whether or not he had anything to do with the decoration of the Meeting House clock is not known. The silver communion service is also of Newport manufacture: there is a chalice by Nicholas Geoffroy, and a flagon and plate by Calder.

Another of the early houses that stood on Thames Street near the Gidley, Redwood, and Malbone houses was built by Richard Munday in collaboration with Benjamin Wyatt. The contract to build this house was signed by them in 1739, and the specifications are still in existence, in the Newport Historical Society. The house was a typical Newport structure, with a central chimney and a gambrel roof. But what was not usual was the hood protecting the front door. This was a feature introduced in England toward the close of the seventeenth century, where later examples were carved in the form of shells or were filled with fruit, flowers, acanthus leaf, or amorini. In Newport, these hoods were extremely rare, used, as far as is known, only on John Coddington's house, on

*Above: A mantel from Godfrey Malbone's town house is now in a room setting at the Newport Historical Society. This, and an ornate carved capital from the front doorway (right), are all that remain of the mansion.*

Above: Interior of the
Sabbatarian Meeting
House, first home of the
Newport Historical
Society. Above the
pulpit is the paneled
sounding board. Left
and opposite: A clock by
William Claggett faces
the pulpit. The
fashionable chinoiserie
designs on the clock
have motifs similar to
those on the lacquered
panels in the Vernon
house.

*Top: Silhouette portrait of the Wood family, painter unknown (collection of the Newport Historical Society). Above: Hood from the Daniel Ayrault house, which once stood on Thames Street. Opposite, above and below: The John Coddington house, 2 Marlborough Street, before and after restoration. Its elevation above commercial premises in effect became an exercise in practical preservation.*

the house Munday or Wyatt built for John Wickes in Warwick, and on the Daniel Ayrault house, which no longer stands. The specifications carried details for its construction. The Ayrault hood may be seen today at the rear door of the Newport Historical Society.

Governor John Coddington's house, at 2 Marlborough Street, was built about 1730 and had a hood, carved by John Stevens, added in 1737. The restored house now carries a hood drawn from the Ayrault hood, as Stevens is known to have modeled his work in this case on Munday's. The handsome house, with interior arches and a curved staircase installed toward the middle of the nineteenth century, retains its early woodwork on the upper floors. The rooms in the gable for many years formed a fourth story, for the entire house was raised about 1900 to make room for a commercial operation at street level—the first example shown in this book of a common Newport exercise in pragmatic preservation.

A two-story house at 40 School Street belonging to James Sisson, an innkeeper, is recorded on the Reverend Stiles's 1758 map; it was probably eighteen to twenty years old when he made note of it. The house was small, with a flat-headed central doorway, and was probably little altered until late in the century, when a new owner, Caleb Green, put on a raised gambrel roof, a fine stairway, and some elegant interior trim. Later still, in the first half of the nineteenth century, the front of the gambrel was raised to form a half-monitor, thus allowing space for a ballroom on the third floor, and the Greek Revival exterior trim, portico, and cupola were added. These changes were probably the work of Lieutenant Governor Charles Collins, who purchased the house in 1823 and brought it into line with the latest architectural styles. It is pleasant to see how the work of these three distinct periods have blended into a distinguished final building.

Captain John Warren's house, at 62 Washington Street, is located in what is known as Easton's Point, or simply the Point, an area granted to Quaker proprietors who divided it into lots in the early 1700s. The Goddards and Townsends, William Claggett, and other shipmasters and craftsmen had their homes and shops on Washington Street (then Water Street), overlooking the wharves and ships that served them. The Warren house stands opposite the end of Poplar Street, on the water. It is a two-story house, with twin chimneys and a gambrel roof pierced by dormers. It was enlarged later in the century, and probably received its fanlight door at that time. Within, the ramped staircase shows typical detail executed in a neat and workmanlike manner. It is a dignified house, suitable for a prosperous sea captain in his time ashore. During the Revolution it served as headquarters for the French Naval Artillery.

*Top: The Sisson-Collins house, 40 School Street. Its present exterior effect largely dates from the early nineteenth century. Above: The dining room.*

*Above: Alcoves flank the fireplace of the Sisson-Collins dining room. Left: The top-floor ballroom.*

Out on Harrison Avenue, south of the center, stands the Brenton farmhouse on Hammersmith Farm. It was built about 1720 on land granted to William Brenton, one of the original settlers of Newport and later governor of the Rhode Island colony. Hammersmith Farm was also the site of Brenton's great 1641 "House of Four Chimneys," which had to be taken down after the Revolution because of the sorry state to which it had been reduced while serving as a military hospital for British troops.

Brenton's farming operations were extensive. In addition to the usual livestock, he ran more than a thousand sheep, and also raised fruit for the market on a large scale. He is credited with having been the first developer of the Rhode Island Greening apple. One of the chief points of interest about the farmhouse is its brick end walls, for stone was still far more common in this application. The original fireplace, only three feet high in deference to the climate, is six and a half feet long. Although the house is not large, its long, low profile (it is only a story and a half under the gambrel roof) gives it an appearance of considerable size when viewed from the front. Lovingly restored and carefully maintained by a succession of private owners in this century, it is still well supported on unchamfered summer beams that measure sixteen by ten inches in section.

Godfrey Malbone, whose Thames Street house rivaled the finest in Newport, was a man who enjoyed his wealth. His way of life was considered lavish in what came to be seen as a lavish era. In 1741 he completed a country house to complement his town mansion. It stood near Miantonomi Hill, about a mile from the waters of the harbor. The short-lived building was destroyed in 1766 by a fire which started in the kitchen chimney one fine July evening when Malbone was entertaining. It seemed to many an appalling loss.

*Opposite: The Captain John Warren house, 62 Washington Street, ca. 1736. Below: The Brenton farmhouse, Harrison Avenue.*

*The late Dr. E. D. Vere Nicoll's team of hackneys, put to a stagecoach, at the Brenton farmhouse. This photograph was taken during the 1978 Newport Carriage Rally.*

Richard Munday, who certainly had a hand in building the now vanished town house mentioned earlier, very likely contributed to the design of the country seat as well, but he did not live to see construction begin. Malbone is said to have spent the immense sum of £20,000 on Malbone Hall, including in the total the cost of the interior fittings. It was built of pink sandstone brought from his own quarry in Connecticut, picked out in white paint at quoins and windows to resemble marble. It carried a sheet-lead roof with a large cupola. Three stories high above a raised basement and situated on rising ground, it must have presented a most impressive appearance to the approaching visitor, who had to ascend a flight of fifteen steps to enter the front door. But Dr. Alexander Hamilton, while describing it as "the largest and most magnificent dwelling house I have seen in America," did not think much of its architectural pretensions, terming it a "clumsy Dutch modell." He admired, rather, the formal gardens and the extraordinary view of Newport and its harbor. Munday's essays after the style of Wren were already outmoded among those who embraced a more refined classicism; Malbone's "splendid country seat" was behind the fashion before it was completed. Nevertheless, it was long remembered by those who had lived in the neighborhood as "the most elegant building in the State."

The 1739 Colony House, which stands at the head of Washington Square, is a splendid example of Munday's work. He received £25 for "draughting a plan" for the building, and looking at it now, one feels that even by the standards of the day, it was cheap at the price. Munday left his stamp on a good deal of Newport's early eighteenth-century architecture. In the last fifteen years of his life (he died in 1740), he produced two triumphant public buildings, which happily still stand.

*The 1727 John Hancock house, Beacon Hill, Boston, demolished in the nineteenth century. It is shown here in an 1831 engraving from a drawing by Alexander Jackson Davis. One of the most elaborate New England mansions of the period, it may have been in some respects the model for Malbone Hall, of which no pictorial record survives.*

*Above: Malbone.
Alexander Jackson
Davis's drawing for the
south elevation of the
Gothic Revival house
built in the nineteenth
century within the ruins
of Malbone Hall. One
of the first Newport
"cottages," it survives
today with few
alterations, save for a
north wing added to
provide a larger dining
room and service
quarters. Sandstone
from the ruins was used
in its construction.*

The Colony House is of brick, with a rusticated basement and belt course of stone from Godfrey Malbone's quarry. The peak of the roof is cut off to form a balustraded balcony, which supports the cupola. The flattened roofline and the truncated pediment give the building an air at once impressive and curiously primitive. For many years the Colony House dominated the Parade (now Washington Square, and always the heart of the city), as it was intended to do; it is unfortunate that later buildings have been allowed to tower over it. From the balcony, the succession of George III was announced, and the Declaration of Independence read to the citizens. The General Assembly of Rhode Island, first of the Colony and then of the State, met there until the final move of the capital to Providence.

*Above: John Stevens's shop, 29 Thames Street, ca. 1760. Stevens carved in both wood and stone; he built the shop to house his marble works. The Stevens family had at that time been masons and stonecutters since 1705, installing foundation walls, steps, and paving; extant account books list bills for whitewashing interior walls. The shop belongs to John Stevens's descendants, and in recent years was the studio of John Howard Benson, the calligrapher. Left: Gravestone carved by the first John Stevens in the Common Burying Ground at Farewell and Warner streets, in a photograph taken by Richard Benson, the son of John Howard Benson and many times great-grandson of Stevens.*

*Right: Doorcase of the John Dennis house, 65 Poplar Street, at the corner of Washington Street. It is a reconstruction of the pineapple doorway that was moved back and forth between this house and the Hunter house several times in the nineteenth century. Below: The John Dennis house today. Moved back on the lot by Charles Follen McKim in 1876, it has lately been restored to its original soft brown color. It is the rectory for St. John's Church.*

*Above: The "Queen Anne" living hall of the Dennis house. McKim moved the stairs into an alcove. The long, low fireplace opening is original. Right: The Parade in the 1840s. Shown from left to right are Charles Feke's house, Pitt's Head Tavern, the Buttrick house, the Mumford house, and the Colony House.*

Opposite: An early-morning photograph of the Colony House, by Samuel Chamberlain. Left: The entrance to the Colony House. James Moody carved the pineapple in 1784, but the rest of the doorway is characteristic of the first half of the century. Below: Assembly Room of the Colony House.

During the Revolution it was a British barracks, and afterward a French hospital, and a good deal of repair was necessary after these incursions. Later changes were made in the nineteenth century, but in 1917 the building was partially restored to its original condition, under Isham's guidance.

Later partitions were removed from the ground floor, which now consists of one immense room with a single row of paneled columnar supports down the middle. The staircase is very fine, with splendid carving. There were formerly three rooms on the *piano nobile:* the Council Chamber, the Middle Room, and the Chamber of Deputies. The last two were joined together in 1843 to make the House of Representatives Chamber, designed by Russell Warren, and given a not unattractive compartmented ceiling. The room has ranges of stick-back benches, which present a handsome effect. Isham was much criticized for not attempting to restore this floor to its original layout, but to sacrifice a good early Victorian interior in favor of two conjectural Colonial rooms would surely have been wrong. The old Council Chamber is the best room in the house, and contains panels and moldings in the style that Hitchcock has designated "Charles III." Originally unpainted and probably stained to resemble a dark wood, the room was painted in 1784, the same year that Jim Moody carved the naturalistic pineapple for the balcony pediment. One of the "Lansdowne" portraits of Washington by Gilbert Stuart, in a very elaborate gilt frame, dominates the room.

If the Touro Synagogue contains Peter Harrison's finest interior, his masterpiece as regards the elevation is undoubtedly the Redwood Library. It is the earliest temple-form public building in North America, only followed nearly half a century later by Thomas Jefferson's Capitol at Richmond. The origins of the library go back to the founding in 1730 of a Newport Literary and Philosophical Society (Dean

*Above: John R. Newell's lithograph of Newport Town and Harbor, from a 1730 overmantel painting.*

Berkeley was a founding member). In 1747 it was decided that a public library should be constructed for the benefit of the community. The impetus was provided by Abraham Redwood, who offered £500 for the purchase of a library of "Arts and Sciences." A great-great-uncle of his had founded the Bristol Library, now the oldest in England in continuous use since its founding.

Abraham Redwood's father and namesake was a sea captain, born in England in 1665; his mother, Mehetable Langford of Antigua, was an heiress. The Redwoods were Quakers, and in the 1770s the Quakers had vowed that no man should hold in bondage a fellow human being. They worked on persuading their members to free their slaves, and a committee called on Redwood to bid him comply. His fruit and sugar plantations in Antigua were entirely dependent on his

*Opposite, above:
The Captain William
Read house, 58
Thames Street, ca.
1740. The gambrel end
faces the street. The
house has an
outstanding staircase
that is ornamented by
turned balusters and
graceful scrolls believed
to be the work of one of
the Townsends. Below:
The Henry Peckham
house, 67 Thames
Street, coeval with the
Read house. Here also
the roof is set end-on to
the street, although the
hip beneath the gable
tends to disguise this.
The other end of the
gambrel is plain;
perhaps the house was
not as large as had
originally been planned.*

slaves, however, and in 1775 he was read out of Meeting. He died in 1788. Although his wealth was ill-gotten by the standards of his fellow Quakers—and by our standards as well—few men have left a monument of such lasting usefulness for posterity.

The sum of £5,000 was subscribed for a building to be erected on the plot presented by Henry Collins. In 1748 a contract was signed with Joseph Harrison, acting on behalf of his brother, who was at that time in London. Upon Peter Harrison's return, the specifications were modified somewhat, in the interests of economy, and the work proceeded. These specifications, which survive in their entirety, are the only existing ones that relate to any of Harrison's Newport buildings.

The original building contained one large room, with a smaller wing on each side, which served for the books, the librarian, and the readers. At one time the chimney of a stove protruded through one of the windows, and in 1791 the librarian was allowed to keep a cow or a horse on the grounds but "no hogs." In 1776 the British officers commandeered it as their club room, and in 1779 many of the subscribers left with the British transport ships for New York, among them the librarian, the Reverend George Bisset, who was also rector of Trinity Church. These Loyalists would hardly have approved the erection of the statue of George Washington which stands before the main entrance today.

In 1858 George Snell added the Reading Room, reusing the three original Palladian windows from the east wall on his new south wall and duplicating them on the north side. A further addition, designed by George Champlin Mason in 1875, became necessary as the library and the demands upon it grew. Isham carried out a thorough restoration in 1915, when among other things the glazing bars were replaced.

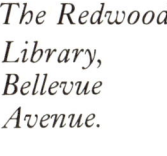

The Redwood
Library,
Bellevue
Avenue.

The Redwood Library.

At the suggestion of Wilmarth Lewis, the Walpole scholar, the 1764 catalogue of books in the Redwood Library was recently republished, along with a request for the replacement of volumes since lost. Enormous interest was aroused among well-wishers, who scoured the bookshops of England and America with notable success. As many as 637 out of the original 751 books are once more on the Redwood shelves.

The Redwood Library and Athenaeum, as it has come to be called, has a collection of pictures and furniture of exceptional interest. Paintings are hung to the ceiling. There is a portrait of Abraham Redwood by Samuel King, who taught Gilbert Stuart to paint. Stuart was born just across the bay, and his first human portrait commissions (Mr. and Mrs. John Banister, executed when the artist was nineteen) hang here. Peter Harrison's portrait, by Louis Sands after Smibert, was painted in 1756, and hangs alongside. There is a Stuart self-portrait, as well as paintings by Lawrence and Sully. Of local interest is Reuben Moulthrop's painting of the Reverend Ezra Stiles, who served two terms as librarian. Stiles's manuscript map of Newport is preserved in the library. There is a self-portrait of Michel Corné, the French artist known locally for his marine views and murals, one of which was executed on the floor of his bedroom. His house still stands at the corner of Mill and Corné streets.

There is also a good collection of Newport furniture. Most sought after by dealers and collectors are the dark green Windsor chairs, the cross stretchers and spindles which are of a unique design, and presumed to be of local origin. In 1885 Miss Ellen Townsend presented some wooden trays made by her grandfather, similar to those used as tabletops. She also gave the library Mrs. William Redwood's card table, which has some obvious Newport characteristics. The recessed block front and open claw feet have been described as

*Opposite, above: The Redwood Library in an early engraving by W. Roberts, before the first alterations and additions were made in 1858. Opposite, below: Grandfather clock made by William Claggett. Left: Mrs. William Redwood's card table. Below: Windsor chairs. All are in the collection of the Redwood Library.*

"probably the finest known on any piece of American furniture." The grandfather clock, made by William Claggett in 1732, is evidence of the exceptionally high standard of craftsmanship attained here at this early date. The japanned case has at one time been shortened, so the clock is now displayed on a plinth to bring it up to the original height. It tells the day of the week and the hour of high tide as well as the time; a cord can be pulled to hear the hour strike to the nearest quarter. The oldest American flag, the Colony flag—authorized by James I in 1606, delivered to Governor Benedict Arnold in 1663, and used until 1779—is historically the most important single item in the collection.

Iron links from the chain that was put across the Hudson to prevent the British from sailing up it are displayed in the library portico. Beside them is a wheel from the earliest train in the United States, which ran on the Charleston and Hamburg Railway. These items bear testimony to the wide variety of interests catered to in this extraordinary collection.

Some neighboring land was bequeathed to the library in 1934, and John Russell Pope was engaged to lay out the grounds. He placed the Redwood Summer House, which once stood on Abraham Redwood's Portsmouth farm, at the end of a long vista of shrubs, and laid down the flagstone walks. The iron main gates leading to Redwood Street were sent from London in 1731 for the Abraham Redwood house on Thames Street; those of the Old Beach Road entrance are modern. They were copied from a pair of wrought-iron gates at Colonial Williamsburg, and forged by Frederick Johnson, a local smith. Of the many rare trees and shrubs the finest is the Fernleaf Beech, imported from England in 1835 and now grown to a height of seventy feet.

The Redwood Summer House, possibly designed by Peter Harrison in 1766, was brought to the library in 1916. Abraham

*Abraham Redwood's house on the farm in Portsmouth.*

*The summer home of William Redwood, Abraham's half-brother. Built by Governor Joseph Whipple about 1745, this large gable-on-hip-roofed house still stands at Two Mile Corner. A thicket separates the remainder of the front lawn from the modernized King's Highway, or Great Road.*

Redwood, Jr., had purchased part of the original Coggeshall holding at Portsmouth and made a garden, installing a greenhouse and a "hott house" for fragile plants. Roots and seeds came from his Antigua plantation and from London, and a gardener was engaged to supervise the operation. Harrison was commissioned to design a suitable summer house from which the garden might be viewed. On November 9, 1766, Redwood's son wrote from England: "I hope you will finish the summer house soon. I flatter myself that I shall spend many agreeable hours with my Father in that pleasant and happy situation. . . ."

Like the library, the Summer House is wooden, rusticated, and sanded to resemble stone. It is a sophisticated building, inspired by a plate in one of Harrison's many architectural books. Harrison probably began acquiring his library in the 1740s; by 1766 he had an extensive and representative collection. After his death, his widow claimed damages for items destroyed by riot, among them furniture, pictures, clothing, "and a large and elegant Library of Books containing to the best of my remembrance between Six and Seven Hundred Volumes, besides Manuscripts and a large Collection of Drawings, all of which were destroyed by a Riotous Mob in 1775."

Some of the volumes could have been local in origin, for Newport had a growing printing industry early in America's history, beginning with James Franklin's establishment of a press here in 1727. That same year he printed John Mammett's *Vindication*, an account of the author's conversion to Quakerism. In 1728, four years before his half-brother Benjamin's *Poor Richard's Almanack* made its first appearance in Philadelphia, James inaugurated his own almanac, *Poor Robin*. By the end of the century, religious works, almanacs, pamphlets, and newspapers were being published by more than half a dozen Newport printers,

*Opposite, above: The Hunter house, 54 Washington Street, in 1870. A stereographic view of the waterside by J. A. Williams shows the pineapple doorway in its original situation. The stair is lit by two segmental, headed windows, and there is a balustrade on the roof. Below: The Hunter house from the waterside, as it appeared in the 1880s. The doorway was removed when the porch was added, and one circular window lighted the stair. The mullions had been taken out of the windows, in typical Victorian modernization, and the balustrade had disappeared from the roof.*

including James Franklin's son James, who founded *The Newport Mercury* in 1758.

The designers responsible for the Hunter house in its final form are unknown, but, as we have seen in other Newport dwellings, the blend of successive tastes and styles has achieved a happy result. The details of the woodwork are highly individual in character, and it seems probable that the woodwork was executed by men trained by Richard Munday in the 1730s. The names of Sheffield, Nichols, and Wanton are associated with the building and evolution of the house, but it was bought by William Hunter in 1805 and did not change hands until 1854, when it ceased to be a private residence. As Hunter was the last private owner, the Preservation Society of Newport County, in whose possession it now is, calls it the Hunter house, and since anything seems better than a string of names attached to a single building, the Hunter house let it be. In spite of the vicissitudes through which the house has gone, more or less following the rise and fall of the fortunes of Newport itself, a remarkable interior has survived; it is the best example in the area of a sophisticated paneled interior of the mid-eighteenth century. The keen interest of a local committee, including such experts as Ralph E. Carpenter, Jr., author of *The Arts and Crafts of Newport Rhode Island 1640–1820*, and the late Lloyd Hyde, has ensured a sensitive and intelligent restoration. Thanks to their generosity and that of their friends, a superb collection of Newport furniture has been acquired for display here, some of it having been returned from as far away as Scotland. An inventory with valuations of Jonathan Nichols's household effects, taken at the time of his death in 1756, shows the contents to have been of a high order then; today the quality of the furniture is beyond praise.

It was the Hunter house that spearheaded the founding, in 1945, of the Preservation Society of Newport County.

*Above: The Hunter
house today.
Right: Detail of the
pineapple doorway.*

*Above: The central hall of the Hunter house. One of the elliptical arches to be found in many Newport houses divides the space.*
*Left: It is possible that this staircase, now in the Hunter house, survived the fire at Malbone, and was installed here when the house was enlarged.*

*Above: The northeast parlor of the Hunter house. Right: An enigmatically cheerful cherub from the carvings above the northeast parlor cupboard.*

Left: The southeast parlor, where the wood is grained to resemble walnut. Over the fireplace is the first commissioned portrait by the young Gilbert Stuart; Dr. William Hunter's spaniels are the subject. Below: A Newport side table in the house.

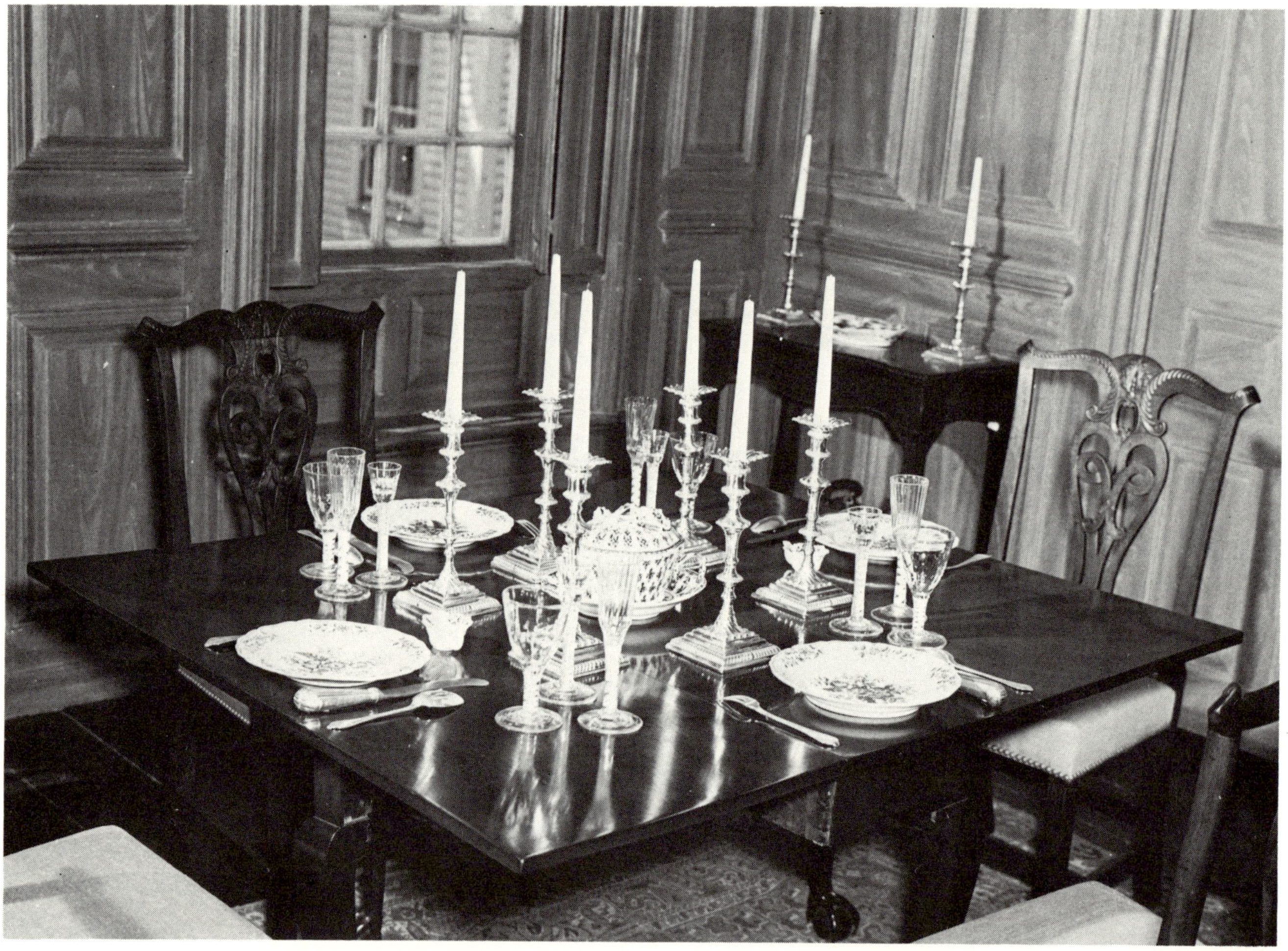

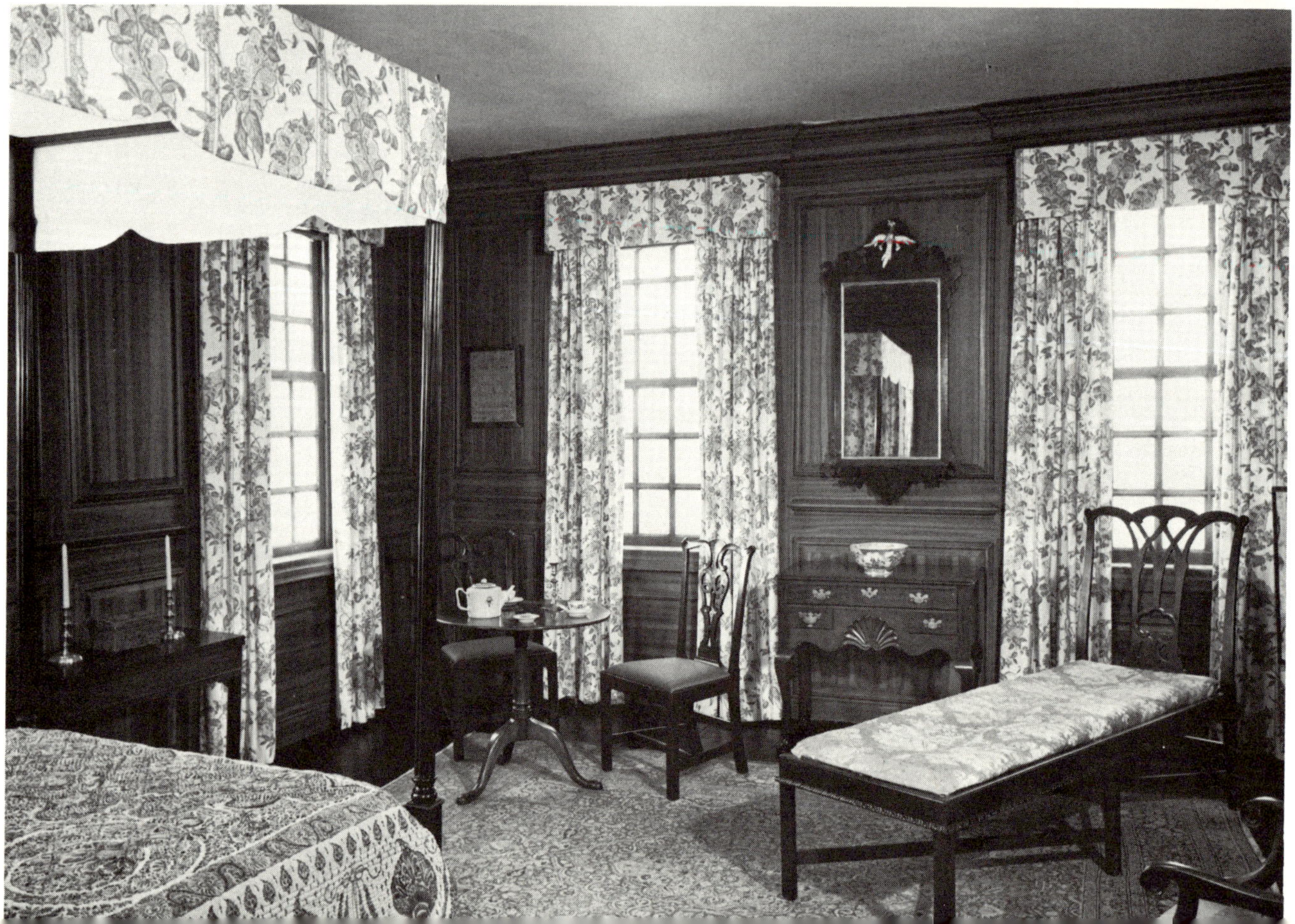

*Opposite, above: The dining room of the Hunter house. Its paneling is grained in imitation cedar; the chairs are of Newport manufacture; and the curved and pointed ornament in the center of the crest rail is almost a Townsend-Goddard signature. Below: The northwest bedroom overlooks the harbor; it is the "Master's" bedroom.*

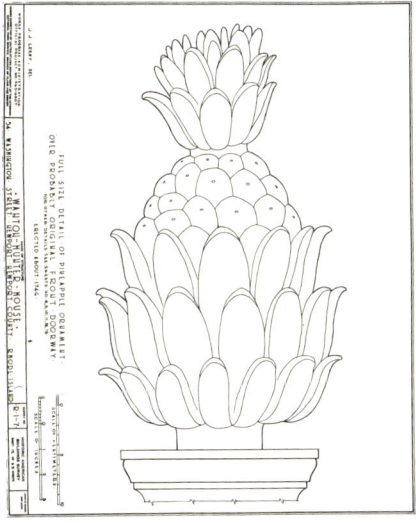

*Detail of a pineapple ornament.*

The Metropolitan Museum of Art in New York planned to purchase the house and to remove the paneling for reinstallation in the American Wing. Mr. and Mrs. George Henry Warren, John Perkins Brown, Wilmarth Lewis, Maxim Karolik, Mrs. Archbold Van Buren, and the Misses Wetmore organized the society in order to purchase the house. They then planned ways to safeguard Newport's many other early buildings, and Antoinette Downing was asked to make a survey of Newport's early architecture.

The history of the building itself is confusing and, because of the lack of documentary evidence, is still open to argument. In 1719 the property where the present house stands was given by one Nathaniel Sheffield to his son who, in 1748, sold it to Deputy Governor Jonathan Nichols, who built the original house. Nichols died in 1754, and in 1756 the property was bought by Joseph Wanton, Jr., who was also to become deputy governor and who is thought to have doubled the house in size. It is evident from the Nichols inventory that a house of some kind stood here by the time of his death, and it is probably incorporated in the present structure. The magnificent staircase with its twisted balusters appears to have been made for another house with higher ceilings. It is typical of the finest Newport joinery of the period, and is part of an elite family to which the staircases at the Colony House, the Sabbatarian Meeting House, and the now demolished David Cheeseborough house of 1737 all belong.

The paneling in the Hunter house has had successive layers of paint removed, revealing that the northeast parlor was originally painted to imitate cedarwood, while the pilasters were marbleized in terre verde. The shell alcoves have been repainted the old green. Winged heads of angels keep watch over the alcoves, and above them the wooden "boxed" cornice breaks forward above the pilasters, the doors, and the

*Above: The Brenton countinghouse, 39 Washington Street. It was built on Champlin's Wharf, Thames Street, but construction of a new road displaced it, making it another in the long list of peripatetic Newport structures. Right: The Newport National Bank, 8 Washington Square, once the home of Abraham Rodriguez Rivera, a leading member of the Sephardic community. The Stiles map shows it as a two-story building with two chimneys; it was probably enlarged after John Gardner bought it in 1722. It has been the bank's home since 1804. Restored in 1950, it is an excellent example of adaptive use in preservation.*

Above: Another example of adaptive use, this building stands just below Touro Synagogue at the junction of Spring and Touro streets. When the corner where it stands became prime commercial property, it was raised, like many of its fellows, to allow for a shop at street level. An outside stair provides access to the original front doorway. Right: Another of these early "houses in the air" stands at the corner of Thames and Coddington streets, just behind 2 Marlborough Street, ensconced above a modern store at street level.

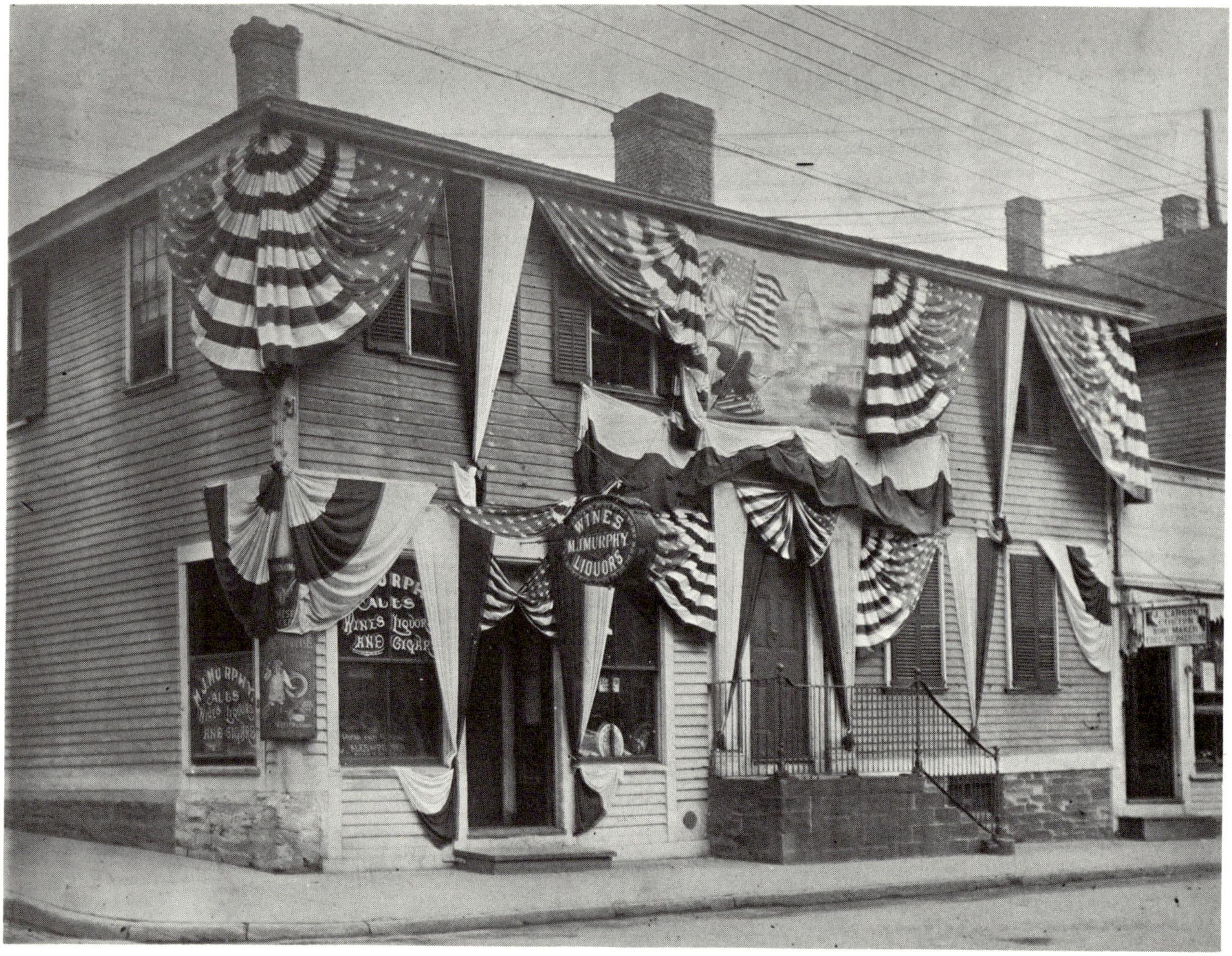
WINES
M.J.MURPHY
LIQUORS

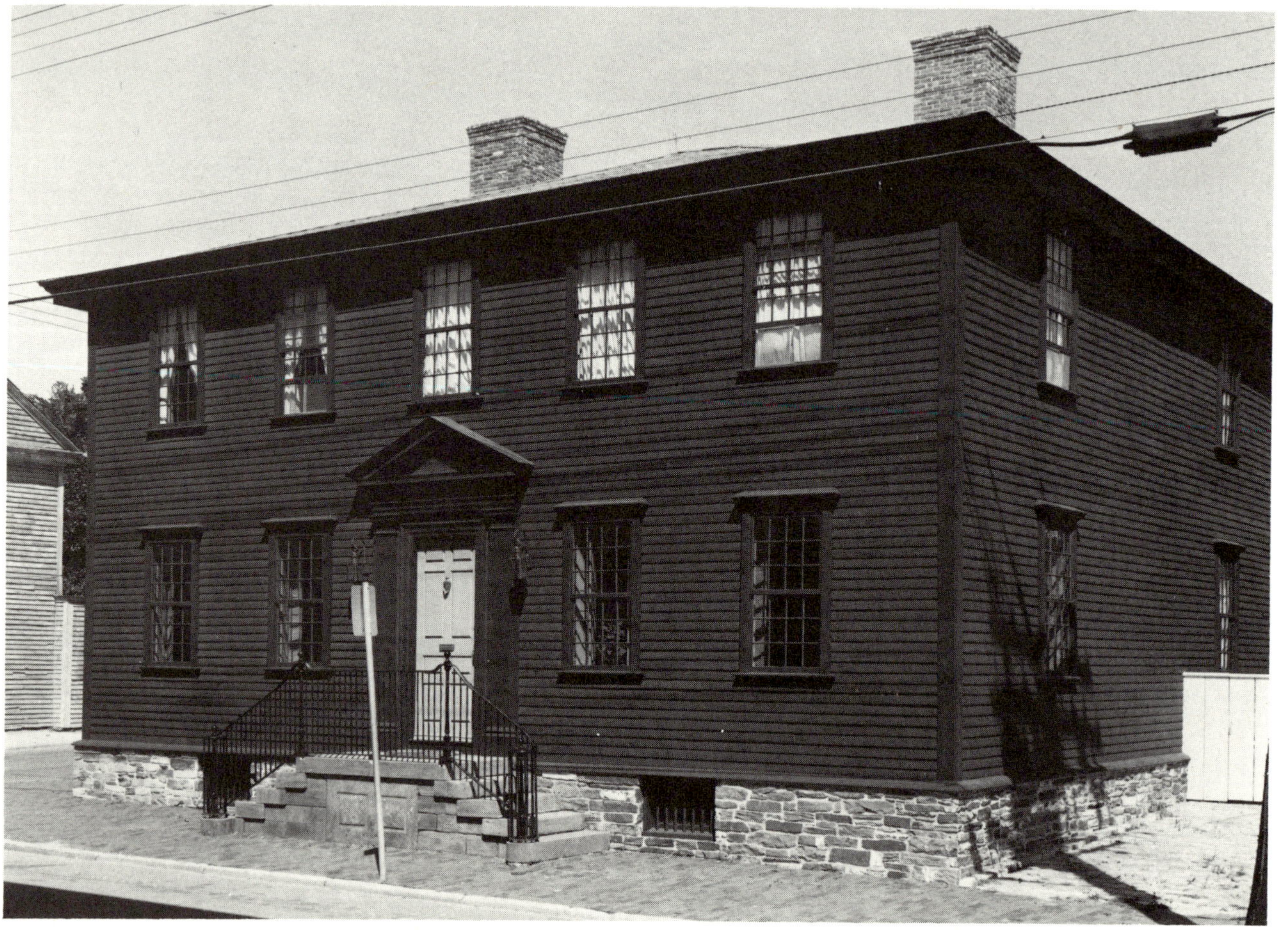

Opposite, above: The Hunter-Whitehorne house, 428 Thames Street, during Old Home Week at the Newport Carnival of 1906. The M. J. Murphy store occupied the north parlor. The house dates from ca. 1750, and follows the usual four-room plan with a central hallway. Below: The house was restored in 1974. It has finely detailed mantels and an elaborate stairway characteristic of the best houses of the period. Above: The Peter Buliod house, 29 Touro Street, ca. 1755. It faces the Green, and has housed the Salvation Army and, earlier, the Rhode Island Bank. The rusticated exterior of wood blocks simulating stone has been restored, and the staircase and some paneling from the demolished Jahleel Brenton house have been incorporated during the recent restoration. Oliver Hazard Perry, hero of the Battle of Lake Erie, lived here in 1808.

*The John Banister house, 56 Pelham Street.*

windows. The proportions of the hearth are wide and low. The mantels have bolection surrounds and no shelf, and the grates are lined in Dutch tiles.

John Banister began to build in 1751 on land that his wife, Hermione Pelham, had inherited from her father. The property had formerly belonged to Governor Benedict Arnold and was known as the Upper Mill Field. Pelham Street goes up the hill from Thames Street, and at the top stands the stone base of Governor Arnold's windmill. Thanks to Banister's account books, 56 Pelham Street, which stands at the corner of Spring Street, is one of the few Newport houses that can be dated exactly. Banister was a prominent merchant who employed the young Peter Harrison both in his business on shore and aboard his ships, but they appear to have fallen out at about the time Harrison proposed to and was accepted by Mrs. Banister's sister, the heiress Elizabeth Pelham. Banister is known to have been a smuggler. He left letters and documents that include both his household accounts and evidence of his heavy involvement in "free trade." He owned warehouses and a wharf on Thames Street, at the foot of Pelham Street, where there was also a dwelling house, doubtless small and old-fashioned. The Pelham Street house (which may, incidentally, have at some time been turned on its lot, as it also was called "the house on Spring Street") is not only spacious, but incorporates the most modish architectural features. It is a large gambrel-roofed structure with two interior chimneys and a central hallway with a coved cornice. A staircase, with delicately twisted balusters, rises at the back of the hall. The lavish paneling of the 1720s and '30s had by then become outmoded, and bolection moldings were no longer used. In the main rooms, the fireplace wall is entirely paneled, but on the other three sides, the paneling only goes up to chair-rail level and is beveled and flat.

*Above and opposite, below: The Prescott (Nichols-Overing) house in an engraving in* Gleason's Pictorial Drawing Room Companion *and as it is today. Left: The parlor of the Prescott house, which has higher ceilings and a grander staircase than most of its neighbors.*

*The John Mawdsley
house at 228 Spring
Street.*

The house remained in the family until 1821, when it was sold to Joshua Sayer; it then remained in the Sayer family until 1906. It subsequently became a lodging house, among other things, but today it is once again a dwelling house, with a comfortable residence in the main section and separate apartments occupying odds and ends of space.

From 1776 to 1779 General Richard Prescott, commander of the British forces in Rhode Island, used the house as his headquarters. This alone is an indication of its importance and elegance—and of the sympathies of its proper tenants. Prescott was domineering, bad-tempered, and highly unpopular. He is supposed to have ordered the removal of all doorsteps that projected onto the pavement so that his officers would not trip over them after a "wet" night; he used the steps to form a walk from the Banister house to the Guard House on Mill Street. Small ladders were hastily set up to take the places of the missing steps, and it has been suggested, not entirely in jest, that the prevalence of recessed doorways in Newport may be owing to Prescott's ruthless gesture.

The Nichols-Overing house, across the King's Highway from Abraham Redwood's Portsmouth farm, was General Prescott's summer residence during the occupation. It was here that he was captured in his bedroom by Colonel William Barton, who had slipped across from Warwick Neck with his officers and some forty men (escaping the attention of no fewer than three British frigates), and readily overcome the single sentry. Prescott was later exchanged and returned to his Rhode Island command, but his temporary discomfiture was balm to the oppressed citizenry of Newport.

The restored 1730 farmhouse is in private hands today, but it overlooks a farm group which is open to the public. This includes various structures that have been moved to the site and are there preserved. The gambrel-roofed Guard House of about 1730 was originally adjacent to the main

*Above: The Knowles-Perry house at the corner of Walnut and Second streets is now much as it was when Matthew C. Perry lived there as a child. Brother to Oliver Perry, he was also a commodore, and was responsible for opening Japanese ports to Western trade. Left: The house before restoration. It was not raised when the store was put into the bottom floor, but an exterior stair was added to give access to the upper stories.*

*Above: A side view of the now demolished John Banister house at One Mile Corner. Right: The front elevation of the Banister country house, now at Winterthur. The façade has been restored to its original brick red, with white cornice, window frames, and door. Note that the door has no outside knob; it was opened only from within, like many another in Rhode Island.*

house; the somewhat earlier Country Store (ca. 1717) was once the ferry-master's house at the Bristol ferry in Portsmouth, and the 1812 windmill was built in Warren, but was moved several times before finding a final haven at the farm.

The John Mawdsley house, at the corner of Spring and John streets, is historically one of the most interesting in Newport, for it bridges the seventeenth and eighteenth centuries (as so many of these old houses do), in a particularly effective fashion, and its rooms hold echoes of voices that still speak to us from the past. The original portion, at the rear, was built in 1680 by Jireh Bull and his wife, Godsgift, daughter of Governor Benedict Arnold. In 1743 the little dwelling was purchased by Captain John Mawdsley, who married a descendant of Walter Clarke, another early Colonial governor, and brought his bride there. Although only twenty-two years of age at this time, Mawdsley had commanded a privateer before immigrating to the New World; in Rhode Island he acquired a fortune and became prominent in Newport affairs.

In keeping with Clarke's position, the early two-room house was enlarged by the building of a two-story addition in front, with the sections joined together by the familiar gable-on-hip roof. The exterior conceals all trace of the earlier building. The façade of the newer structure displays heavily capped windows, a modillion cornice, and three pedimented dormer windows.

At the rear of the central hall, a stairway makes the transition between the earlier and later sections. The south parlor, now the dining room, has elegant paneling, window seats, and inside shutters. A dentil cornice, and the mantel, which is surmounted by an eared panel and broken scroll pediment, complete the decoration of the room. Similar paneling was installed in the north parlor and in the room behind it, which is part of the old house. The Mawdsleys entertained

*Opposite: The Banister staircase and hall at Winterthur. The entrance to the stair hall is a paneled arch, supported on carved corbels and painted its original olive color. Doors, trim, and handrail have been once more stained in imitation of walnut, and the treads retain their old marbleizing, in gray and buff. The mahogany breakfast table is an excellent illustration of the Newport Chippendale style. The cabriole legs, each ending in long claws clasping an orb, were a favorite conceit of John Goddard's. Mid-century chairs combine Chippendale ball-and-claw feet with the solid splat of the earlier Queen Anne period. Right: Chippendale Bedroom at Winterthur, from the Banister house. Only the hearth wall, with its bolection-molding fireplace surround, is fully paneled. The dwarf tall clock has works by William Claggett; the case is probably Townsend-Goddard. The pierced splats of the side chairs are typical of Newport Chippendale; the Newport easy chair has flat stretchers.*

frequently; contemporary accounts record that "hospitality and urbanity marked his steps."

In 1780 and '81 the house was the headquarters of François Jean, marquis de Chastellux, Rochambeau's second in command, who was called by one observer "the diplomat in Rochambeau's army," and who entertained on a scale suitable to his position and delightful to Newport's war-impoverished citizens. The Reverend Stiles, noted for his unaffected way of life, yet entered in his diary on one occasion: "Dined at Gen. de Chastelux in a splendid manner on 35 dishes. He is a capital Literary Character, a Member of the French Academy. He is the Glory of the Army."

Chastellux traveled from Newport to Philadelphia and Albany on his commander's business, keeping notes of all he saw; Part I of his *Travels in North America* was written at the Mawdsley house. First printed by the press of the French fleet in Newport, it has seen several editions in French and English, and is one of our most penetrating and entertaining contemporary commentaries.

Caleb Gardner, a still prosperous Newport merchant, purchased the Mawdsley house in 1795, after the owner's death. Gardner had been a Revolutionary hero and was a friend of Washington. It was he who installed the stylish doorway with its fanlight, and he probably imported the marble steps and walk at the same time. Later owners further embellished the house; Theophilus Pitman introduced the mantels from the Benjamin Pitman house on Broadway when it was demolished. It was owned for a while by The Society for the Preservation of New England Antiquities, and has also served as the Girl Scout headquarters. It has recently been purchased by Mr. and Mrs. Frank Ray, who are restoring it. Once again Captain John Mawdsley's house, created in the best taste of his day, is a home in the true sense of the word.

John Banister had two houses in the country, at One Mile Corner, in addition to his town house on Pelham Street. One of these was burned by the British, but the other, built about 1756, survived until the 1950s. It had a gable-on-hip roof, and there were two interior chimneys serving the rooms on either side of the hall that ran through the center of the house. As at the Hunter house, the hall was divided by an arch setting off the elegant stairway with twisted balusters at the rear. On the landing, an arched window gave light to both floors. The wooden exterior was rusticated to resemble sandstone. This, together with the stair window, has led to the belief that Peter Harrison had a hand in the design, but although he was Banister's brother-in-law, they were, as has been noted, not on good terms. However, the house is of approximately the same date as the enlarged Vernon house, and there are similarities in the detail at both residences.

John Banister's house was altered through the years, fell vacant, and was

*Above: A cupboard in the Robinson house that is part of the original woodwork. Right: The dining room occupies the sunny southeast corner of the earliest part of the house.*

*Above: The Robinson parlor, "Colonialized" in 1872. Right: The Townsend-Goddard secretary, in the Great Room added by Thomas Robinson.*

To be SOLD or LET, by

# Col. Job Almy

## Of TIVERTON,

A LARGE commodious new dwelling Houfe, well finiſhed, and painted blue; fituate at the upper End of Thames Street, near Capt. Jofeph Wanton's. A Stable, Garden, and good Well, belonging thereto, with a fine Cellar, and other Conveniencies. Whoever inclines to view faid Houfe, may apply to Capt. Job Snell, or Mr. Conftant Bailey.

*Above: A 1758 advertisement for the Almy-Taggart house (see page 19).*

demolished in 1956. The façade was installed at Winterthur in Delaware in 1963, along with the stair hall and a bedroom, which are furnished with Newport pieces to demonstrate the patrician life-style of a prosperous, mid-century Newport merchant. These, together with additional Newport furniture elsewhere in the museum, emphasize the impact of that city's eighteenth-century craftsmen on the plastic arts of this country.

At about the same time that the Banister house was under construction, the Almy-Taggart house, at 56 Farewell Street, was being enlarged and remodeled. The nucleus of the house dates from about 1710, but it was expanded to the rear, and by 1758 had reached its present dimensions and final character. For many years, shingles covered the blue horizontal siding, with its unusual beaded edges. (Blue was always a highly popular color in Newport.) Over the years, the house sustained many interior alterations, but the rather fine staircase remained in place, and has supplied a point of reference for the restoration work. The central chimney, which provides seven fireplaces on three floors, has been restored.

The Robinson house faces the water on Washington Street. Like the nearby Hunter house, it at one time had its own wharf, and a shop and other outbuildings shared the lot. Its situation was ideal for the supervision of cargo coming or going, and in 1760 "Quaker Tom" Robinson, a prosperous merchant, purchased the modest original 1725 house, and extended it to the north to obtain additional space and elegance. It remained unchanged thereafter for many years, and the eventual Victorian alterations respect its scale and character. Charles Follen McKim "Colonialized" the kitchen in 1872, providing a sitting room overlooking the harbor, thus effectively turning the living quarters to face the waterscape; the obligatory shady Victorian porch was added at that time.

*Touro Synagogue,*
*Touro Street.*

A Tuscan Altar Piece.

Opposite: The interior of Touro Synagogue, looking east. Above, left: The ark. Above: A Tuscan altarpiece from Langley's Treasury of Design. Left: Historic American Buildings Survey drawing of the first-floor plan.

In 1780 the vicomte de Noailles, Lafayette's brother-in-law and an officer with the French expeditionary force, was billeted with the Robinsons. The vicomtesse sent a Sèvres tea set to the family along with a delightful letter of thanks for their kindness to her husband. The tea service and letter are still in the house—which has not passed out of the family—together with pieces of Newport furniture that in two hundred years have moved no more than the few hundred feet from the shops where they were crafted. (The vicomtesse later perished under the guillotine of the Terror.)

There had been a Jewish congregation in Newport for a hundred years when Touro Synagogue was built. The community was founded in 1658 by a group of Sephardic Jews from Spain and Portugal; they met for worship on the Sabbath in one another's houses. An additional sixty Jewish families arrived in 1755, subsequent to the Lisbon earthquake, and in 1758 Isaac de Touro emigrated from Amsterdam. His was the driving force behind the establishment of a permanent place of worship. Touro Synagogue was dedicated in 1763. Peter Harrison appears to have produced the design—as a favor, since there is no record of his having received any payment. It is built of red brick, painted cream with chocolate trim, and the exterior gives no warning of the beauty within, for it is without doubt the best interior that Harrison designed.

It is laid out in the traditional Sephardic manner, with seats for the men around the perimeter and an upstairs gallery reserved for the female members of the congregation. The gallery is supported by twelve Ionic columns, symbolic of the twelve tribes of Israel. From these spring Corinthian columns, which in turn support the ceiling. The effect is grand yet intimate. Harrison drew on architectural pattern books for the detail, but the arrangement was his own invention,

*Above: The Francis Malbone house, 392 Thames Street. An early photograph, showing the window caps still in place. Right: Another view of the Francis Malbone house, as it is today.*

*The Cozzens house,
57–59 Farewell Street,
ca. 1765. It faces the
blue Almy-Taggart
house, forming a
pleasant entrance to the
Farewell–Thames Street
area. It holds two
separate residences
under the same gambrel
roof, and is one of the
better examples of the
eighteenth-century
double house. Lately
rescued from a sad state
of dilapidation, it has
been beautifully
restored. Opposite: 1758
map of Newport, by the
Reverend Ezra Stiles.*

ingeniously adapted to the requirements of Jewish custom.

The decoration around the ark, which appears to be plasterwork, is in fact carved wood painted. The upper half contains a primitive canvas representing the Ten Commandments and is signed "Benjamin Howland, Pinx, 1828." Indeed, there is some confusion as to the date of the whole configuration of the ark because of a sketch in Ezra Stiles's diary (reproduced in Antoinette Downing's *The Architectural Heritage of Newport, Rhode Island*) that shows an arrangement of cupboards with segmental heads surmounted by a panel with Hebrew texts. Dr. Stiles made the sketch at the dedication of the synagogue in 1763, when the building was barely ready for the ceremony. It seems probable that the ark he sketched was a portable one that had been transferred from house to house—panels with segmental heads were widely used in Newport during the 1730s. For the permanent installation of the ark as it is today, Harrison borrowed from Batty Langley's *Treasury of Design* (1750), and the frame of the Ten Commandments above was taken from James Gibbs's *Rules for Drawing.*

Among the treasures preserved within the ark are some ancient scrolls ornamented with elaborate tops that were made in 1765 by Myers and Hays, New York silversmiths. The ark faces east, toward Jerusalem; this accounts for the angle at which the building rests on its site.

After the post-Revolutionary collapse of Newport's economy, the Jewish community dwindled and the synagogue was closed, but fortunately its future was guaranteed by Abraham Touro's 1832 bequest. The building was kept in repair, and, more important still, its architectural detail was not tampered with, as must have happened had it been converted to another use. Abraham's brother Judah established a ministerial fund in his will, and, in the 1880s, with the return of a measure of

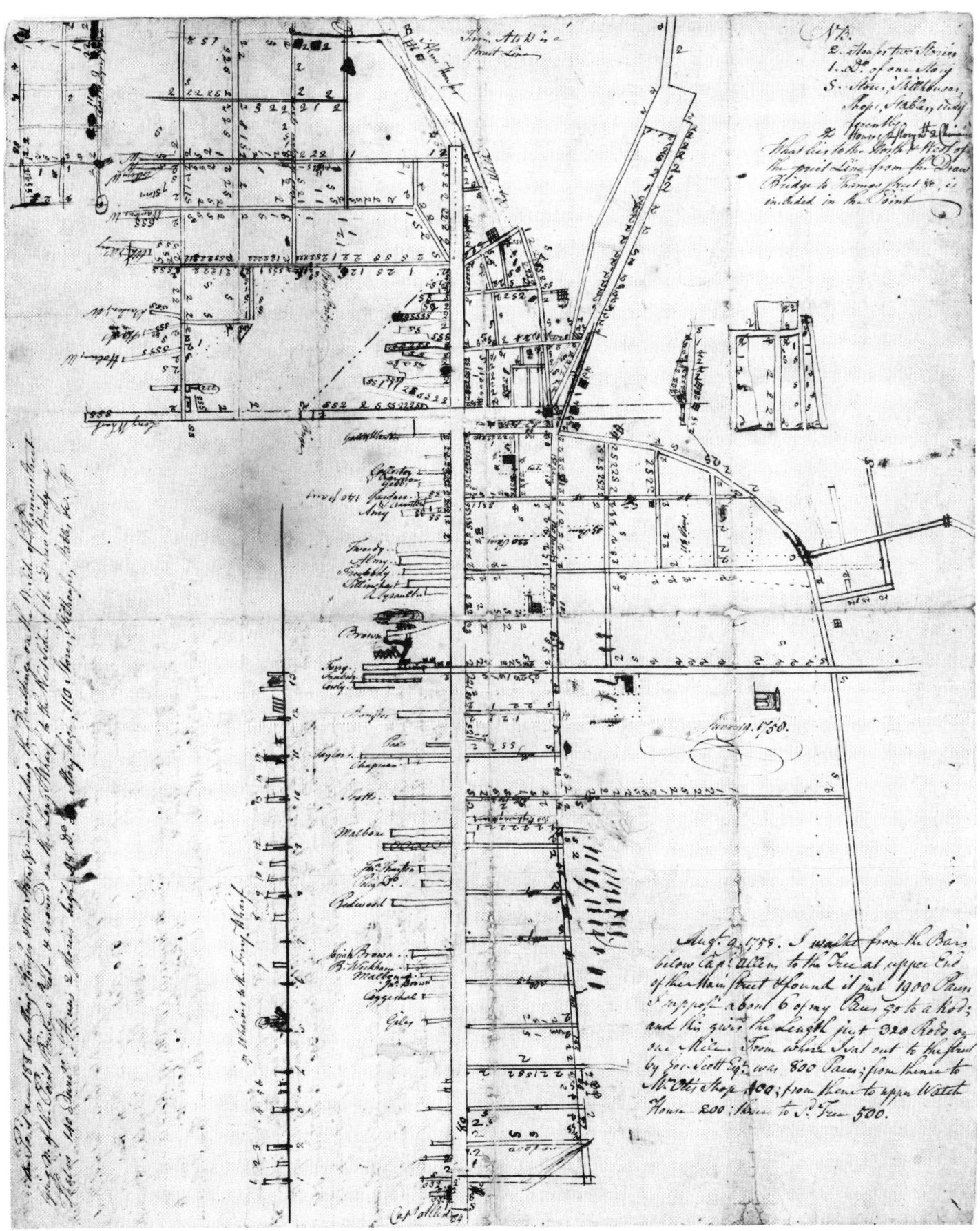

prosperity to the town, the synagogue was reopened for worship.

Further restoration work was carried out for the two-hundredth anniversary of the synagogue in 1963, although it was decided not to strip the paint off the exterior for fear of damaging the old brickwork. The woodwork had many coats of paint, and the present gray color was carefully matched to the first of these. Reproductions of eighteenth-century Windsor chairs were acquired, and the old wooden floor was carpeted to deaden noise. Rabbi Theodore Lewis, from Dublin, was in charge of these improvements. In 1972 he established in the annex the George Washington Museum Room, which is devoted to the early Jewish settlement in Newport.

The Francis Malbone house stands on Thames Street between Young and Brewer streets. It is the last survivor in its immediate neighborhood of the mansion houses that faced the harbor. Most were built on the east side of Thames Street, while the warehouses, the stores, and the wharves were situated on the waterside.

Francis Malbone was a cousin of Godfrey Malbone, and, like him, a merchant and slave trader. He purchased the lot in 1758 and work doubtless soon began on his new house; the architectural style is characteristic of the mid-century. It is possible that Peter Harrison designed the house, but no records have yet surfaced to confirm this. It is known, however, that Samuel Greene and Wing Spooner, two of the carpenters who had worked for Harrison on the Redwood Library ten years before, also worked here.

This is a remarkably early example of the style of "owner's houses" seen in many seaports along the Atlantic Coast, especially in New England, for most structures of similar design and scale date from the close of the eighteenth century and the early Federal period. The plan is typical; there is a broad central hall with two rooms on each side. Two chimneys serve the fireplaces in these

Extends 131.
a Scale of 60 Feet.
The Elevation of the Great Gallery in SOMERSET House to the River.
Is most humbly Inscribed to the Right Honble the Earl of OXFORD &c. My Lord High Treasurer of Great BRITAIN, Knight of the
most Noble Order of the Garter &c:
Elevation de La Grande Gallerie Del' Hostel de SOMERSET du costé de la Riviere, est tres humblement Dedié a Monseigneur Le Cont D'OXFORD &c:

*The Brick Market, at
the west end of
Washington Square
(formerly the Parade).*

rooms; the Malbone house was built with a full third story instead of garret space, so there are four more fireplaces than usual. The third story emphasizes the kinship of the house to the town mansions of such cities as Salem and Newburyport. Another similarity is the adjoining countinghouse, built in the 1850s for a doctor's office.

The hall is divided into two by an elliptical arch supported by brackets; the stairs at the rear, with their twisted balusters, are lit by a round-headed window. The front parlors are paneled on all four walls and have dentil cornices. There are two-story pedimented mantels in both parlors, with the one in the north parlor carrying a broken scroll. A similar arrangement is found at the Vernon house.

Vicomte Desandrouins, the commander of the French Army's Engineering Corps in Newport, was quartered here. In 1827 the family sold the house. Joseph Totten of the U.S. Army Corps of Engineers, who was stationed in Newport for the rebuilding and enlarging of Fort Adams and who purchased the house in 1833, was the first of a number of further owners; in 1910 the house became St. Clare's Home. Recently the Francis Malbone house became the residence of Mrs. Elizabeth Morris Smith. She has embarked on a restoration program embracing both the house and the office, but the heavy window caps on the front, which can be seen in old photographs, have yet to be replaced.

The Long Wharf was at the center of the original Newport settlement, at the foot of the Parade. It was one of the main watergates to the town. Stiles's 1758 map shows the wharf at a broad crossroads, still in the center; by this time the Colony House dominated the head of the Parade, but the market had not yet been built.

In 1753 the Long Wharf Proprietors voted that "liberty be granted the applicants to erect a market house where the upper

*Above: The restored Billings-Coggeshall house, ca. 1784, at its new location at 35–37 Mill Street. It is composed of two independent sections, each with its own entry, stairway, and chimney. Extra space on the second floor was gained by bridging over the passage to the rear court. Right: The John Townsend house and workshop, 70–72 Bridge Street. Many houses built by early craftsmen survive in this area.*

*The Denman house, 6 Elm Street. It was moved to its present site from the corner of Charles and North Baptist streets. This little house, with its central chimney and gabled roof, dates from the mid-eighteenth century, but the fanlight doorway was put in at the end of the century, when even modest residences received fashionable embellishment.*

*Right: This small house at the top of Prospect Hill is one of the less imposing residences which add to the townscape and are still being restored. Restored in 1979, it modestly turns the end of its gambrel to the street, presenting a three-story façade with entrance steps that intrude onto the pavement. Below: The staircase, still in its original position, awaiting the attentions of carpenter and painter.*

watch house now stands." Nothing was done until 1760, when the Proprietors set aside land on Thames Street for a market, "the upper part to be divided into stores for dry goods" and "the lower part thereof for a Market House, and for no other use whatsoever forever (unless it shall be found convenient to appropriate some part of it for a watch house). A handsome brick building, to be thirty-three feet in front or in width and about sixty-six feet in length." By the tenth of July a committee had been appointed to confer with Peter Harrison, by this time the architect of the Redwood Library, Touro Synagogue, Christ Church in Cambridge, and Kings Chapel in Boston, among other achievements.

Peter Harrison's own architectural library provided inspiration for the Market. At this time in England a favorite scheme was a high arcaded basement supporting the structure above. In Colin Campbell's *Vitruvius Britannicus* of 1716 Inigo Jones's design for Old Somerset House appears; Fiske Kimball suggests that the original source was not Palladian but Michelangelo's Palazzo Senatorio in Rome.

Harrison took the Jones design as his model, but altered the detail. Brick was substituted for stone, in keeping with the Proprietors' directive, and the window design was simplified, with the Ionic order substituted for the Corinthian. The Brick Market has been accounted one of Harrison's finest essays.

The interior has been greatly altered. The lower part was used both as a watchhouse and as a market for a number of years, and the two upper floors were let for shops and offices. Just after the Revolutionary War it was used for a printing office. From 1793 to 1799 Alexander Placide rented this part as a theater; there may still be seen a fragment of one of the theatrical scenes: a seascape with ships, painted directly on the plaster of the east wall.

*Opposite: The Rogers house, 37 Touro Street, ca. 1800. A nice example of the transition to the Federal style. In structure it follows the style of mid-century three-story houses, but the detailing is more refined. The doorway, with its Corinthian columns, is the principal feature of a rather understated elevation.*

The Market was altered in 1842 to serve as a town hall. The floor of the third story was removed to make one huge room upstairs, with galleries on three sides. Windows and doors filled the lower arcades and the area used for stores. From 1853 to 1900 the building served as a town hall, and was afterward put to various civic uses.

In 1928 the exterior of the structure was restored under Isham's direction, sponsored by Mr. John Nicholas Brown. The ochre paint which had been applied in the nineteenth century was removed, and the bricks on the north and east basement walls, which had deteriorated, were replaced. The arcades remain closed in with small-paned windows, but otherwise it is as Peter Harrison designed it: a handsome market in the English academic taste of the time.

An urban-renewal program was embarked upon in Newport after the Second World War, and much of the area about the Brick Market below Thames Street was gutted. In the open space thus created, the Market can be seen on all sides. A mall, which approximately follows the line of the Long Wharf down the north side, prolongs the vista from the Colony House, so that the view is as it was before. The area has been one of mixed development—shops, restaurants, housing, a marina—so that at all hours of the day and night there is activity. After two centuries the Brick Market still presides over the multifarious activities of a busy waterfront.

A South-West View of Newport, *an August 1795 engraving in the collection of the Newport Historical Society.*

# *EPILOGUE: AFTER 1800*

A S WE HAVE MENTIONED, NEWPORT lost more than half its population during the British occupation; by the close of the eighteenth century there were no more than four thousand residents in the community—hardly more than there had been in 1700. Many important citizens were among the exiles, for influential persons of known Revolutionary sympathies often found it expedient to withdraw from under the shadow of the Crown and most Loyalists prudently left with the departing British garrison.

It must not be supposed, however, that Newport became a ghost town. Some merchants returned to reestablish coastal trade in a limited way. There was even a brief revival of the slave trade, and the fertile surrounding farms, although depleted of timber and often denuded of buildings and fencing as well, once again began producing meat and produce for distant markets. Nor had all the craftsmen vanished. Their work was in widespread demand, although their production was somewhat limited for want of materials.

Samuel Whitehorne was a shipping magnate involved in a number of commercial enterprises, including a distillery, an iron foundry, and a bank. He was probably also active in the slave trade. In 1811 he built a fine three-story Federal mansion at the corner of Thames and Denison streets. Laid out on the familiar Colonial four-room plan, it is constructed of brick and carries a hip roof. The central hall is divided into two spaces by a broad elliptical arch, like that in the 1750 Hunter house. The staircase rises from the back of the hallway, and there are two rooms on either side.

The front door with elliptical leaded fanlight and sidelights, the arched center

*Facing Touro Park and the Old Stone Mill, Warren House, at 118 Mill Street, was built in 1809, carrying into the new century the three-story tradition of the earlier Francis Malbone house. For many years the summer home of Mr. and Mrs. George Henry Warren, it is now the headquarters of the Preservation Society of Newport County.*

*Above: The Samuel Whitehorne house, 416 Thames Street, pictured about 1890, when two shops had been introduced into the ground floor. Right and opposite, above: When the shopfronts of the Samuel Whitehorne house were removed, the western façade was exposed for the first time in many years. Opposite, below: The Whitehorne house in the 1980s.*

*Above: The southwest room of the Whitehorne house; work in progress. Right: The room at the start of the restoration.*

*The southwest room,*
*now the dining room.*

*Above: The parlor of the Whitehorne house. The mahogany Chippendale block-and-shell chest-on-chest is attributed to the Townsend-Goddard family. It was made between 1760 and 1780. The mahogany chairs of the same period are attributed to John Townsend. Right: A kneehole chest of drawers in the parlor carries the ogee brackets with scrolls on the inside edge that are peculiar to Townsend-Goddard work. This is one of the finest pieces of Newport furniture still in existence.*

*The southwest bedroom. The mahogany Chippendale bonnet-top highboy, made in two parts, dates from ca. 1760–80. It has descended in the Lyman Hazard family of Peacedale, Rhode Island, and tradition has it that the piece was ordered from John Goddard. The Queen Anne tea table, ca. 1740–60, is also a Townsend-Goddard piece. The cabriole legs end in slipper feet, a common Rhode Island convention.*

window above it, and the top-floor bull's-eye window combine to emphasize the early Federal character of the front. Dentil cornices and reeded chair rails add to the decorative interest of the interior, and there are carved wood panels in the chief rooms. The furniture presently in the house is almost entirely of Newport manufacture. Combined with local silver and pewter work, it creates an air of elegance and warmth appropriate to the house and its period.

Whitehorne went bankrupt, having lost two ships at a time when his credit was overextended, and his house was sold at auction in 1844. Later owners allowed it to deteriorate: an early addition housing shops stretched right across the front; the ground floor was cut up by partitions; and the rooms above were divided into a warren of apartments. In 1974 the house was acquired by the Newport Restoration Foundation. The cupola, which had been added around 1850, was retained, but the remainder of the house has been returned to its original configuration. Together with its garden (which reflects the horticultural interests of the time and contains rare varieties of gooseberries, grapes, peach trees, roses, and tree peonies imported from China), it is open to the public. Garden and house form a fine example of a gentleman's establishment of the early Federal period.

Berkeley's "star of Empire" was beginning to take its "Westward" way, and the bustling port city was soon transmuted into a sleepy seaside town, overshadowed by its humming naval base and rapidly becoming a mecca for summer visitors. Until the Civil War, many Charlestonians took ship to Newport in order to escape the steamy South Carolina heat. The cozy but spacious townscape, with its examples of what was already "quaint" architecture, the charm of the views over the harbor and the open ocean, the local associations with Revolutionary history, and the modest cost of comfortable lodgings, combined to attract a seasonal colony of artists and literati seeking fresh air,

*The* Hercules Courtenay, *painted in 1802 by an unknown artist.*

HERCULES COURTENAY of NEWPORT Cap HENRY HUDSON

inspiring scenery, and a quiet life. Hotels and boardinghouses prospered, and to a degree service businesses took the place of the sterner industries of the previous age. The acme of this resort era was reached in the latter part of the nineteenth century, when Newport was "taken up" by the moguls of monied Society.

The Newport of Ochre Court, Marble House, and The Breakers was crippled by the First World War, just as Malbone and Redwood's Newport had been crippled by the Revolution. Both survived after a fashion, but the impetus was gone; the grand summer palaces came to be symbolic of a past that now seems only a trifle less remote than the earlier history embodied in the old town.

Thousands now pass through Newport every year to enjoy the scenic amenities that struck its earliest visitors, and to admire the artifacts and architecture of earlier generations. The importance of tourism to the prosperity of the town has improved the lot of the preservationist, for the city fathers are fully aware of the attractions of their period buildings. This spirit of cooperation between public and private interests, while by no means always unflawed, has made ambitious restoration projects feasible. Without it there would be no Queen Anne Square.

One of the great challenges of restoration work, beyond determining the original structure and identifying what is often a series of alterations and accretions, is to ascertain what parts of the fabric can be saved, what must be replaced or reproduced, and how best to coordinate new and old work so that the building maintains its integrity and character. Sometimes only fragments of an early structure have been preserved, to be introduced into settings in which they are appropriate. Newport preservationists have been notably successful in this aspect of their work.

Another obstacle that has to be surmounted in such places as Newport is the now impractical situation of some buildings

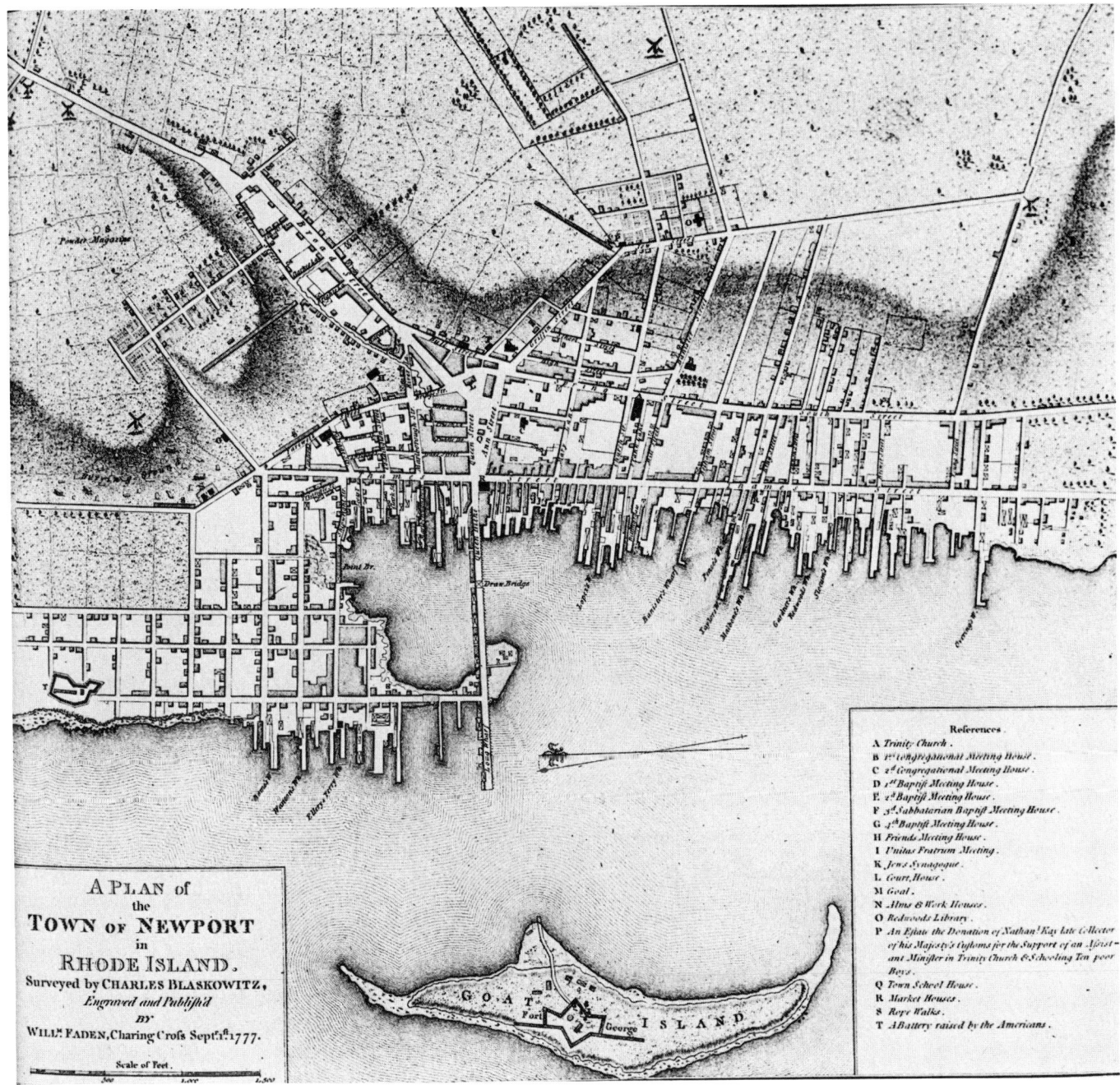

A PLAN of
the
TOWN of NEWPORT
in
RHODE ISLAND.
Surveyed by CHARLES BLASKOWITZ,
Engraved and Publish'd
BY
WILL.ᵐ FADEN, Charing Cross Sept.ᵗʰ 1777.

Scale of Feet.

References.

A  Trinity Church.
B  1ˢᵗ Congregational Meeting House.
C  2ᵈ Congregational Meeting House.
D  1ˢᵗ Baptist Meeting House.
E  2ᵈ Baptist Meeting House.
F  3ᵈ Sabbatarian Baptist Meeting House.
G  4ᵗʰ Baptist Meeting House.
H  Friends Meeting House.
I  Unitas Fratrum Meeting.
K  Jews Synagogue.
L  Court House.
M  Goal.
N  Alms & Work Houses.
O  Redwoods Library.
P  An Estate the Donation of Nathan.ˡ Kay late Collector
   of his Majesty's Customs for the Support of an Assist-
   ant Minister in Trinity Church & Schooling Ten poor
   Boys.
Q  Town School House.
R  Market Houses.
S  Rope Walks.
T  A Battery raised by the Americans.

GOAT      ISLAND
Fort George

*The pineapple, traditional symbol of hospitality, is a familiar emblem in Newport. Carvings, old and new, are found on fence posts as well as over doorways.*

demanding rehabilitation. This difficulty has been overcome by moving a number of dwellings to new sites, at once concentrating a large number of protected buildings in a single accessible area and removing them from busy commercial sections, where the land is too valuable and the traffic too heavy to allow for the enjoyment of charming anachronisms. At first sight the uprooting of ancient structures might seem ruthless, and contrary to archaeological truth, but in so doing the perpetrators are only following an old New England custom, which has been a commonplace in Newport for a very long time. Downing has described the framing of the earliest houses as being "... expert and self-sufficient as the stone vaulting system of a Gothic church." This braced and framed system of construction survived long after baroque and classical influences had modified and concealed the massive components. It is comparatively easy to move such a structure as a unit, to turn it on its lot, to elevate it so that a new ground floor may be inserted, or to transport it to another site. Baron Ludwig von Clausen, in his *Revolutionary Journal*, writes of Newport:

> A frequent practice that would seem rather extraordinary to those who have not seen it, is that of transporting the wooden houses, which are built on stone foundations, completely intact from one quarter to another, and even into the country; the framework, just as it is, is placed on some little wagons attached to each other. I have seen some, drawn by 30 or 40 oxen or horses.

The Rhode Island legislature has not met in Newport for more than a hundred years. The naval base is quiet now, and the great merchants who founded their fortunes here and the later tycoons who brought the wealth acquired elsewhere to build the mansions along the Cliff Walk have alike passed into history. Nowadays the name "Newport" evokes thoughts of the America's Cup races, of rock and jazz and chamber-music festivals,

of agreeably instructive summer walking
tours. There is even a brand of cigarettes
called Newport; the word connotes the
pleasant dissipation of leisure hours. But as
we admire the strength and variety of its
architectural heritage, let us not forget its vital
and glorious past.

*The Common Burying
Ground at Farewell
and Warner streets.*

# *A*CKNOWLEDGMENTS

In the beginning, the authors very much wish to thank their editor at Viking Penguin, Mary Velthoven, who has pressed on undismayed throughout this, our third book together; our gratitude also to Jacquelin D. J. Sadler for her contributions to the finished product.

The staffs of various Newport organizations have been unfailingly helpful in supplying material and answering our endless questions.

We, the authors, and we, the public, should be eternally grateful to the late Katherine A. Warren, who, back in 1945, helped found the Preservation Society of Newport County, and for the remainder of her life devoted much time and effort to the cause of preservation in Newport. Her former home is the headquarters of the society—a most appropriate example of preservation by adaptive use. We wish to thank Society President John G. Winslow; Director Paul E. Molitor, Jr.; Mrs. L. J. Pannagio; and John Cherol.

At the Newport Restoration Foundation our thanks go to President and Director Doris Duke, to Manager Peter S. Kent, and to James Potter, George Weaver, Ron Little, Judy Boss, and Clementine Lalli.

At the Newport Historical Society we are obliged to Mrs. Peter Bolhouse, Mrs. Edmund H. Wardell, Christopher LaRoux, and Jean Vibert, and, at the Redwood Library, to Donald T. Gibbs and Richard L. Champlin. We are also grateful for the assistance of Rabbi Theodore Lewis of Touro Synagogue, who, like Bishop Berkeley, came to these shores from Ireland.

Our appreciation for timely tips, advice, and diverse facts must go to Thomas Tew Benson; Ralph E. Carpenter, Jr.; the late J. A. Lloyd Hyde; Jacqueline Onassis; John F. Millar; John F. A. Herzan; Betty Ring; Nancy Sirkis; Narcissa Chamberlain; and David O. Merrill.

A special thank-you to Alan Pryce-Jones for the warmth and shelter of the little house that brought us into a personal relationship with the eighteenth-century Newport we came to study. Further information, companionship, and hospitality in our leisure moments were offered by Richard Banks; John Barrington Bayley; Mrs. John Howard Benson; Mrs. Stanford F. Brent; Mr. and Mrs. Claus von Bülow; Mr. and Mrs. Ralph E. Carpenter, Jr.; Margaretta Clulow; Mr. and Mrs. Robin Corbin; Min Cushing; Mr. and Mrs. John R. Drexel III; Doris Duke; Beatrice Greenough; Mr. and Mrs. Patrick G. Kirby; Anthony Kloman; Mrs. Alexander Liggett; Mrs. Quinto Maganini; Mrs. Bingham W. Morris; Captain and Mrs. Jack C. Myers; Audrey Oswald; Senator and Mrs. Claiborne Pell; Mr. and Mrs. Frank Ray; Benjamin C. Read; Mr. and Mrs. T. J. Oakley Rhinelander; Mr. and Mrs. Alan T. Schumacher; Mr. and Mrs. John J. Slocum; Elizabeth Morris Smith; the Countess Szapary; the Reverend Henry G. Turnbull; Gypsy Vanderveer; Mr. and Mrs. Henry Austin Wood, Jr.; Henry A. Wood III; Joan Wood; and Mr. and Mrs. Edwin P. Young. Our thanks to all!

Profound gratitude and admiration to Richard Benson, Robert Foley, and John Hopf, photographers-in-residence of Newport, who are always at the right place at the right time, with the right filter and shutter speed. . . .

Finally, the authors wish to extend very special credit and wholehearted thanks to Gladys Bolhouse, Richard Champlin, and Antoinette Downing, for so generously lending their expertise during the preparation of *Newport Preserv'd.* Any omissions or errors in this volume are emphatically not the reponsibility of these kind and knowledgeable scholars.

# INDEX

*Page numbers in italics refer to pages with captions.*